D1480705

Among
the
Anti-
Americans

Books by Thomas B. Morgan

Friends and Fellow Students
Self-Creations: 13 Impersonalities
This Blessed Shore (a novel)
Among the Anti-Americans

Holt, Rinehart and Winston
New York
Chicago San Francisco

Among the Anti-Americans

ASBURY PARK PUBLIC LIBRARY
ASBURY PARK, NEW JERSEY

Thomas B. Morgan

Copyright © 1967 by Thomas B. Morgan

All rights reserved, including the right to reproduce
this book or portions thereof in any form.

Published simultaneously in Canada by Holt, Rinehart
and Winston of Canada, Limited.

Library of Congress Catalog Card Number: 66-13208

Acknowledgment:
Portions of my chapter on Indonesians appeared in a different form in
Life Magazine and *The London Observer;* the visit to Hiroshima described
in my chapter on the Japanese was published in *Venture* Magazine, also in
a different form.

First Edition

Designer: Ernst Reichl
85830-0217
Printed in the United States of America

This book is for
Kate, my daughter,
and Nick, my son

15860

Contents

"*I am willing to love all mankind, except an American.*"
Samuel Johnson: Boswell's Life

"*Between knowledge of what really exists and ignorance of what does not exist lies the domain of opinion. It is more obscure than knowledge, but clearer than ignorance.*"
Plato: The Republic

Among
the
Anti-
Americans

1
Introduction

Travel strengthens the conviction that the world is full of people. It is also necessary for anyone interested in the historical fact that so many of them today are antagonistic to the United States.

So I took a trip not long ago, going 45,000 jet miles in nineteen weeks. I traveled from New York to New York via Brazil, Japan, Indonesia, Egypt, Kenya, and France to find out what I could about the grounds for anti-Americanism abroad. I had decided to avoid the Soviet Union because I felt that ideological anti-Americanism, used by a communist state as an instrument of foreign policy, could just as well be left to specialists at home. Half way along I realized that this was nonsense and yearned to peel off into Eastern Europe. By that time, however, I had spent the advance from my publisher. Someday, I hope to verify for myself that the Russians are really there.

I want to emphasize that the building of friendships and mutuality between Americans and the rest of mankind was going on apace wherever I went. One of the most hopeful things I found was the warmth and the feeling of community that existed among United States scientists and artists, students, businessmen, and journalists, and their non-American counterparts.

At the same time, there were certain sour issues that had antagonized almost everyone abroad, regardless of nationality.

These include our race crisis and the war in Vietnam, the memory of McCarthyism and the unforgettable assassination of John F. Kennedy, the workings of the Central Intelligence Agency and the tragic inadequacy of our global economic policies. Above all, virtually the whole world seemed to have had about enough of what was once a good thing: our post-war interventionism. Abroad it sometimes appeared that we had extended the Monroe Doctrine to cover the earth, far beyond the requirements of a rational balance-of-power policy. We were accused of a new kind of isolationism, of going it alone in the world without that "decent respect to the opinions of mankind" that Jefferson bequeathed us. In the long run, I think our current preference for lonely, do-it-yourself diplomacy may be as damaging to our national interest as our old isolationism was in the pre-Pearl Harbor past.

With all this, anti-Americanism remains one of those abstractions on which politics thrive—one of the symbols, in Walter Lippmann's phrase, "by which public feeling is for the moment contained." It is a means to various ends. Probe for the motives of anti-Americans and you are (or, at least, I was) confronted by the chaos of the human condition. I asked hundreds of people how they felt about us and why. Many replied in terms of self-interest. Some explained by telling me their life history. Opinions flowed on geopolitical strategy and the limits of love. There was a Japanese girl who just kissed me. And when I met Sukarno, I lost interest in anti-Americanism while viewing his really heroic self-indulgence. Getting to know him necessarily posed the question: to what extent are all of us responsible for the personal whimsy and eccentricity of our leaders? In short, now that I am back, I usually think of my sojourn among the anti-Americans as an improbable adventure that proved Alexander Hamilton's thesis: "The causes of hostility among nations are innumerable."

In a way that I shall never forget, I also learned that all men feel hate, exasperation, and friendship in much the same way. Perhaps you and I would be among the hostiles if we lived in any of the countries I visited.

Under the circumstances, it is natural to want to do something about the situation. And we can, in time, if there is time. We can improve our "image"—perhaps through less dependence upon advertising and public relations techniques. We can refine our energy and conserve our wealth. And we can submit a portion of our power to international control. But, while we wait on change, paying a little more attention to what people abroad are saying and what they mean when they say it may help us live in the world with a little more grace.

2
Brazilians

On the morning of December 7, 1964, flying down to Rio de Janeiro, I had my first glimpse of the Brazilian coast, emerald green trimmed with buff, seen momentarily through a patch in gray clouds heavy with rain. The young man across the aisle had seen it, too, and we fell to talking. He was an M.D. from Des Moines, Iowa, on his way with his wife and three children to spend six months in Bolivia on a community health project. His specialty was schistosomiasis, a dysentery transmitted by snails in water, that ravishes Latin America, Asia, and Africa. He said the cure was not even to wash clothes in the water, let alone drink it. He sounded so hopeless, I asked him why he had accepted the assignment.

"It must help our image for them to see someone that cares," he said.

Later on, a man named Sanchez chimed in. He was a cork merchant in Rio, returning from a business trip to New York. A tuna-fisherman in his spare time, he said he often fished the south Atlantic off the eastern shore fifty miles north of his city.

"The landscape there hasn't been spoiled by Coca-Cola signs," he said.

I did not believe we were supposed to take offense at that, but he seemed to think we might and quickly offered to take Des Moines and me fishing any time, *amigos*.

I recall both of them, the American doctor and the Brazilian merchant, because together they helped crystalize my sense of that time. A few years before, the Kennedy-Nixon presidential campaign had raised America's interest in its foreign "image" to the level of a major issue. We called it the "prestige gap," meaning that our power was somehow greater than the world's respect for it. Respect is a nice word used in international politics meaning fear. Then we applauded the Cuban confrontation of 1962 because this momentarily narrowed that gap. And we celebrated President Johnson's 1964 election landslide because, among other reasons, it staved off adverse "world opinion" of a Goldwater victory. Republicans and Democrats alike, we were a nation that tended to accept the language of public relations—and its goals as well. Through some failure in our own self-esteem, there had been a trend in this lonely direction ever since the first election of President Eisenhower (and the defeat of Stevenson). The record of the past twelve years showed, I thought, that neither our support for democratic processes around the world nor our aid to underdeveloped countries were anywhere near as consistent as our concern for our reputation. In part, we were reacting to Communist propaganda. But it seemed indisputable that our conception of national interests abroad reflected distortions of self-interest at home. It followed, as we might have expected, that anti-Americans everywhere in the more or less free world carried on foreign—that is to say, public—relations with the United States in the streets. Thus, Latin Americans spat on our emissaries. Asians, Arabs, and Africans burned our effigies. And Europeans splashed ink on our embassy walls. And so, too, an American doctor set off to conquer dysentery at the risk of five lives. And a Brazilian merchant with clients in New York hastened to dis-offend two American strangers on a plane.

The approach to Rio was as advertised. Narrow shafts of midday sunlight pierced the clouds over the mountains, selecting the most dramatic peaks for emphasis. And behind the great crescent beach, the sprawl of buildings was dappled white, green, and gray.

I spent two weeks in Brazil where, seven months earlier, backed by the Brazilian army and probably by the Government of the United States, General Castelo Branco had overthrown the constitutional regime of João Goulart. An expert at our embassy would argue that there had been no time to impeach President Goulart through due process: "It was Cuba all over again. The morning of the coup, I told my wife to pack our bags because we'd be leaving if Goulart survived." But here we were heavily committed to yet another Latin American dictatorship. Over all was a sense of slow-running time, with intimations of nightmares to come. U.S.-style cocktail lounges, movies from Hollywood, and billboards by Doyle, Dane, and Bernbach impressed me, not because pop culture was more dolefully symbolic here than at home, but because it underscored the contrasts of the city, between rich and poor, old and new, sweet and sour. Rio gave me a feeling of having regressed about thirty years to an American metropolis, circa 1934, surrounded by the countryside, waiting for the Roosevelt revolution, or something.

On my first afternoon in town, I rode a bus to find the setting of *Black Orpheus*. I got off in an industrial neighborhood called San Cristoval and walked until I came to a dead end at the base of a steep hill. Climbing a slender, tangled path, I paused near the crest and looked back. Half of Rio spread out on the plain below. To the east was the harbor crowded with ships waiting for berths. And to the west, on the side of a mountain was the grand mansion of the Roman Catholic Cardinal, Dom Jayme de Barros Camara of Rio. It was strange to be virtually in the heart of the city and yet feel so remote from it. I continued to the top of the hill. Before me, fanning out left and right, and pouring down the far slope, were hundreds of tiny, tin-roofed shacks made of wood or a kind of adobe, some leaning on one another, all under a smoke haze through which the dipping sun looked like a rotten egg. My guess was that ten thousand people lived here, all refugees from Brazil's endemic rural depression. There were a million like them in Rio.

In the *favela* of San Cristoval, ragged children were every-where with their games. Men leaned against shanty walls, passing the time rolling cigarettes or matching coins. There were no women in sight because country women find domestic and fac-tory jobs in the city more readily than their men. In this, the *favelados* are not unlike the captives in Harlem. But in all ways, their lot looked poorer. The idlers I saw seemed to be waiting for the girls to come home from work. One spoke to me in English. He was a gaunt man with bright black eyes and gray skin. No, the inflation did not bother him too much. The cruzeiro was worth about one-hundreth of its 1960 value, but he was getting by. No, he was not interested in politics. "God is a Brazilian," he said. "He lets the politicians sleep at night so that He can correct their mistakes." Great black ugly birds cruised about overhead, occasionally swooping down to snatch at a piece of rubbish. There was the stink of sewage, too, accompanied by the sound of a tuneless guitar. And no carnival.

I dined at my Copacabana beach hotel a few nights later with an intellectual whom I shall call Luis O., inasmuch as I agreed not to mention his name in print. He was a sardonic, fat man who fancied himself a wit. He said he was interested in the problem of America's role, as he put it, "in everybody's business." He had studied in Washington and New York and was writing a book about political trends in the United States. "Everyone in Brazil is interested in American trends," Luis said, "because we are always having to adjust to them. We are very good at adjusting." He stabbed mercilessly at his lamb chop. "We call it *acomodismo*," he said, "which means adjusting to change so that everything stays the same. You Americans may have been right about the Goulart situation. You called him a Castro. But you never ask why, if this was true, there was so little trouble when Goulart was overthrown. Well, it could be that there was no Castro situation. But even if there was, what happened next was perfectly in char-acter. Brazil adjusted, and *poof!* the communist threat, if there was one, disappeared overnight. Of course, the secret police still knock on certain doors, and many people are in jail or exile, but *acomodismo* takes care of everything."

Luis O. looked a little frenzied. Apparently, it relieved him to confess that which he obviously hated most about his country-men. It made him feel guilty, too. For a moment, I thought he might bolt from the table. After he had calmed down, he went on. "*Acomodismo* offers one great advantage over the American way of life. It counteracts the romanticism of false hope. We know here what life is. But you Americans have nothing to coun-teract romanticism, so you don't know. Your companies come here and exploit us. Your C.I.A. and your armies meddle in our politics. And your style of life flows in here on every merchant ship stuffed with cans of film and chewing gum. And yet, you yourself will tell me *you* have nothing to do with all this and that you yourself are lovable. Even the North American businessman wants to be loved. Ha! We, too, want love, but we understand that love is a very rare thing. So, *acomodismo* . . . You *don't* understand, so that is why it is so very easy to fool an American. All we have to do is smile. 'Ah,' the American says, 'I am loved!' You see, I smile at you and I make you feel good. Now, I pick your pocket." Luis deftly snatched a cigarette from the pack in my shirt pocket.

"We have many reasons for hating you, my friend," he said, "but I think we hate you most because you are so romantic. That is worse than paying us criminal prices for our coffee."

Luis smiled and sighed. "Well, won't it all be over in a few years?" he asked himself. "Yes, I think so. You will be fooled into fighting the Chinese. And the Russians will pick up the pieces because they smiled at you. How you enjoyed Senhor Khru-shchev's smile! What you call the *thaw* is his smile. It neatly relieves your European flank so that you can be maneuvered into fighting the Russians' war with the Chinese. Oh, anyone can have his way with you if he knows how and when to smile."

After Luis O. had gone, I went for a walk on the beach. The sky was black and fuzzy above a faint warm mist. Far up on the slopes behind the fine hotels and apartments, I could see the yellow eyes of another *favela*. Two girls wearing T-shirts strolled along with me for awhile. Then they dropped back on another lone beachwalker. The last I saw of them, they were headed up a side street with the new man in between.

Back in the hotel lobby, I bought a newspaper and went upstairs. The news was speculative: Somebody said Castro's repressions in Cuba defeated Cheddi Jagan in British Guiana. Somebody else said the Alliance for Progress, despite its growing pains, would elect Eduardo Frei in Chile. Hard news on the front page consisted of a single story. David Bell, director of U.S. foreign aid, all $3.5 billion of it, had arrived in Rio for talks with President Castelo Branco, economic planning minister Roberto Campos, and U.S. Ambassador Lincoln Gordon. Bell's schedule also included a visit to Recife, capital of Pernambuco State in Northeast Brazil, on December 18, to "formalize" a grant to the new regime. The mayor of Recife would honor him with a ceremonial dinner and reception.

Late on the next afternoon, dashing through the rain, I failed to stop the only empty taxi in Rio. By bus and then on foot, I arrived bedraggled at the home of Sergio Bernardes, who ranks second only to Oscar Niemeyer, designer of Brasilia, among Brazilian architects. Sergio had built his home on a cliff beyond Copacabana beach overlooking the ocean and the city as well. The house was typical of his style, emphasizing burnished colors and the dramatic use of light and shadow within and between the rooms, first to alert and then to relax the aesthetic nerve. Sergio himself was a full, dark, dashing man in his fifties. His wife, though younger and considerably more fragile, was somehow equally dashing. They had two dashing young sons and a gigantic, dashing Doberman.

After dinner, with an arm flung around my shoulder, Sergio guided me into his studio. It was a vast workshop with drafting tables for a dozen men, most of whom were still on the job, polishing his latest commission: a city plan for Rio in the year 2000 A.D. Sergio's use of bridge pylons as living space and of pyramid-shaped skyscrapers designed to allow light and air into a city center appealed to me—although both concepts were reminiscent of the work of Japan's Kenzo Tange, whom I hoped to meet in Tokyo. Sergio released me in order to have both hands free to jab and pound his map of Rio's future. He was most enthusiastic about the prospect of super-intercontinental jets landing here to serve the continent.

"Morgan!" he cried. "South America must become a continental nation! And—*Morgan—Rio* must be the center of the continent!"

Then Sergio grabbed a rough sketch of prospective low-income public housing. "To design a new city," he exulted, "you must respect nature, respect people, use common sense, and determine your motives. . . . So, Morgan—when we design housing, we must let the people who will live in it say more about design. Here you see a framework. Now, we let the people themselves design inside with that *something* the architect cannot have. *They will design with love for their own home!* Yes, Morgan?"

Holding my arm tightly, Sergio walked me back to his living room. It was a long, comfortable space with dark beams, red tiled floors, and glass doors positioned so that one could look through them to the moon-lit ocean and yet see the reflected lights of the city. Here, the great architect unburdened his feelings about the United States. He insisted America should not give money to Brazil. "People resent a giver!" he said. "Better your government should stimulate investments in Brazil by giving income tax benefits at home for Americans who let their money stay here. . . . You see, I admire the *internal* policy of the United States. You have great political stability—marvelous equilibrium achieved by combining conservatism with soaring research. It is marvelous! But *externally*—no! You could change the world, but you don't understand. You think of countries, when it is basic to think of individuals. Yes, study the atom to understand the universe! Then you would see that people always get together if there is an economic motive—and we must get this continent together. . . . You must lead, Morgan, because you are the leading country. You must give up your policy of encouraging the separation of Latin nations and make a new policy dedicated to bringing people together on a continental basis. Technology demands it. Do you hear me, Morgan!"

Sergio sat back, out of breath. He sighed and lit an expensive cigar. Through blue smoke, he said Brazilians were an uncertain race with "know-how" but not "know-when and know-why." Then he smiled and said, "You know, Morgan, after the April revolution, I was interrogated by a military tribunal. They asked me if I was a Red and I said I was not a Red because I have compared Russia and America and decided America is best."

Next morning, the weather was soft and clear. I flew to Recife to see the local archbishop, Dom Helder Camara. I had heard much about him in Rio. He had been in charge of Catholic "social action" under Cardinal Jayme until his assignment to the Northeast archdiocese just after the overthrow of Goulart. Despite the weakness and conservatism of the Brazilian Church, his moral and personal magnetism made him a national leader of progressives, whose antagonism toward Castelo Branco's regime extended to the Americans backing it. Newsmen called him "the electric mosquito."

Since the mid-Fifties, Dom Helder had concentrated on projects and appeals for the *favelados* and the peasant masses, enlisting middle-class *cariocas*, especially women, in Brazil's first mass adult literacy program, its first slum clearance project, and its first welfare service center, which he called the Bank of Providence. Somewhat in the manner of our Fulton Sheen, he exploited radio and television to gather support for his crusades. He was a popular idol and a confidant of three presidents—Kubitschek, Quadros, and Goulart.

When in April, at age fifty-five, he opted for Recife, numerous *cariocas* were glad to see him go. I had mentioned his name to an industrialist named Alberto Faria, who described him as "a salesman, a fake, and a geek." Gustavo Corcao, a conservative Catholic philosopher, told me the man was guilty of "materialism, modernism, pride, opportunism, heresy, toleration of communism

and socialism, and falsehood." Sergio Bernardes called him a
"paternalist." And a political officer at the American Embassy
showed me a photograph of Dom Helder and President Goulart
taken in late March at the height of crisis and widely distributed
as part of the populists' last ditch effort to stay in power: "A few
days later," the American told me, "Castelo Branco summoned
Dom Helder to Brasilia to find out where he stood. Obviously, the
President was satisfied because he let Dom Helder go to Recife.
But *you* be careful."

On the other hand, Dom Helder's admirers looked upon his
transfer as the Church's first sensible answer to the radical peasant league movement in Brazil's Northeast. Unfortunately, this
thesis could not be tested right away because Castelo Branco had
given his own answer first—jailing peasant leaders, including
Francisco Julião, whose style reminded conservatives and progressives alike of the early Fidel Castro; suppressing some of the
more violent leagues; and moving the rest firmly, if not permanently, toward reorientation along less radical lines. Economic
development remained the central issue of Brazilian politics
against a background of misery and factionalism, but Dom
Helder's chance to increase the progressives' influence on public
opinion had been momentarily diminished. Yet, he retained an
enthusiastic following all over Brazil.

Luis O. had said, "Dom Helder is a saint. On television, with
all of Brazil for an audience, he is very strong and understated.
He could teach Billy Graham a few things about mass hypnotism.
He *ad libs* on social action, current events, slum conditions, and
economic problems. But he never, never talks politics—which
shows he has thought about it. He is very subtle. He understands
symbolism. Eleven out of twelve Brazilians know who he is and
respect him. . . . I would like to see him President of Brazil!"

A lumber and paper tycoon, Israel Klabin, one of a small group
of industrialists identified with progressivism in Brazil, defended
him against the charge that he had conspired with Goulart to
save the old regime. "We all knew the overthrow of Goulart had
to happen," Klabin said. "Dom Helder is one with those who

knew but who now oppose the conservative tendency to look upon development as a mere technical process. He sees the priority of human values against the conservative ideology of econometrics. . . . The electronic computer has ended economic ideology. It is neutral. The essence is in priorities, in the decisions you make. Priorities cannot be stated in economic terms. What is needed is social ideology. . . . Dom Helder's point, our point, is that underdevelopment is not caused by economics, but by a lack of appropriate men. This means a greater investment in motivation, in opening the ruling class to many, in bringing greater participation of the people, in encouraging the younger generation to fight for the betterment of society. . . ."

And Elisabete Cardoso, the singer who was to Rio what Edith Piaf had been to Paris, said he was "a transcendental man." She did not believe anyone could hate him.

There was one more thing I had heard about the archbishop of Recife. As a delegate to the Second Session of the Vatican Council in late 1963, Dom Helder had submitted an informal paper entitled "An Exchange of Ideas with our Brothers in the Episcopate." He wrote that an examination of doctrine was less important at that time than a return to poverty. He proposed suppression of such clerical titles as *excellency* and *eminence* and elimination of priestly coats of arms, mottoes, silver-buckled shoes, limousines, grandiose living quarters, and expensive rings and pectoral crosses. "It seems like nothing," Dom Helder wrote, "but how this creates distance between our clergy and the faithful! It separates us from our own century, which has already adopted another style of life. It separates us, especially, from the workers and the poor. . . . There are small and simple cars, the uses of which everyone understands and accepts, and there are cars that scandalize and revolt. Let us not make our moral strength and our authority depend upon the make of the car. . . . Let us end once and for all the impression of a bishop-prince residing in a palace, isolated from his clergy, whom he treats distantly and coldly." Then he asked that all bishops attending the closing mass of the Council place their gold and silver pectoral crosses at the Pope's feet and receive in return a cross of bronze or wood.

Dom Helder's paper raised a minor furor among the Council delegates. But no one suggested he had not practiced what he preached. In Rio since the mid-Forties, he had lived with his mother and spinster sister in a two-room flat.

I stayed three days in Recife, an old, damp city, gray even in bright sunlight, on a peninsula eight degrees below the equator. The local Chamber of Commerce called it the "Venice of Brazil," but there were no canals. Recife is built partly on islands at the intersection of two rivers and derives a faintly Venetian flavor from their connecting bridges. About half a million people were living here and a few had been rich for a long time on fortunes made in land and in exports: mostly cotton, fruits, hides, lumber, rum, and sugar. The other business of the city was politics. Both landlords and peasants skirmishing in the hinterland recognized Recife not only as capital of Pernambuco but as the strategic center in any ultimate struggle for the Northeast.

At my hotel on the edge of town, people sat in the lobby all day and half the night watching television. The news programs were sponsored by ESSO. One way or another, it seemed that TV was available to almost everyone in town. If a man did not have his own, he went to a hotel or a bar or, if he was very poor, stood in the street and watched programs through someone else's window. The cheap transistor radio had caught on, too. I saw a man wearing a turtle shell for a hat driving to market with a feeble load of pineapples in a donkey cart holding a radio to his ear as he passed by the hotel. I could imagine him listening to commercials and wondering why he did not have the money to buy what was for sale or lending his ear to any politician able to speak his language. There was nothing *remote* about Recife.

About two P.M. that first day in town, I found the Archbishop's Palace, Dom Helder Camara's official residence on a tree-lined street in one of Recife's more expensive neighborhoods. Behind an iron gate, broad steps led up to a grimly ornate yellow and pink building. The windows were shuttered against the heat. Two workmen lolled under a shade tree. Insects buzzed in the soggy stillness. It was as though the overpowering inertia of the Church itself had been concentrated within this muggy garden spot.

Through a side door, I entered into a vast murky room where an old nun asked me to wait. A dim painting of the Last Supper hung on one wall and, in the darkest corner, a glass chest displayed old china. Black and yellow floor boards in the classic Iberian style gave off a dull glow under a thick and fastidious coating of wax. I felt like whistling.

After a few minutes, Dom Helder Camara came in from an adjoining room. He was a wisp of a man, about five-four with a few strands of graying hair on his head, which was very wide at the crown and narrowed sharply to a pointed chin. Castelo Branco's head was shaped about the same way. As it happened, both men were natives of Ceará where, instead of rocking babies to sleep, mothers swing them head down—or so I had been told. Some Brazilians believed this accounted for the extraordinary number of intellectuals produced in that state. Dom Helder's face was worn and deeply lined but brightened by large, soulful green eyes. His nose was heavy; his mouth small with a gap between the front teeth. He wore a dusty black cassock and a wooden pectoral cross.

Dom Helder shook hands with a preoccupied grip and greeted me in Portuguese. I had remembered to get a letter of introduction from a mutual American friend, which he read swiftly. Then we went up a marble staircase to a small conference room overlooking the street. Here were eight high-backed wicker chairs arranged in a semi-circle, and no table. We sat side by side. Speaking English, he said I might smoke if I liked; but there was no ashtray. I told him I was at the beginning of a long trip, an effort to reorient myself to reality. He seemed to want to hear my voice before deciding whether to talk to me at all. So, for five minutes, I did my fanciest taps.

The archbishop listened. Then he flattened his tiny palm against his wide forehead, closed his eyes, and compressed himself. In a small voice, he said he had a busy schedule for this day.

"But tomorrow," he said, "I can give you an hour in the early afternoon. After that I am making a TV show; then a special mass in Olinda, our sister city, for a class of graduating architects; then a wedding, a high school graduation, and a reception—a reception for your David Bell and Ambassador Lincoln Gordon."

It was as though he was reading a list off the backs of his eyelids. Then he opened his eyes. "Tomorrow, if you bring me a list of questions, I will write out answers. And if you like, we can have time to talk between the functions of my day. Meanwhile, I want you to know I believe in faith, hope, and love. I believe God wants man to be His co-creator and that He is proud of man's efforts. That is why I shall amass public opinion here for economic development. Through television and every means, I will talk to our little rich man in São Paulo and in Rio who has his money in Swiss banks and Bolivian oil. I want him to see that one cannot have a valid position in regard to the United States and the developed world until industrialized southern Brazil invests in underdeveloped northern Brazil."

Dom Helder stood up. He clenched his fists, saying underdeveloped Latin America was the shame of Christianity. "But this may now be a political blessing for the world," he said. "Latin American Christianity is the only one that did not collaborate with colonialism, so today Latin America can be the bridge to Asia and Africa for everyone's sake."

Dom Helder extended his arm and pointed through the window as though the Church were out there moving in the vanguard of social justice. One understood his appeal for masses of people even if some of his facts were wrong.

Then the old nun came into the room, snapped open an ancient pocket watch, and showed Dom Helder that my time was up.

After lunch next day, I returned to the Palacio and Dom Helder again escorted me to the conference room. It was as before except that a table had been added.

"Read me your questions," he said, "then I will write out the answers. My hand speaks better English than my lips."

He opened a drawer in the table and extracted a pen and a pad of paper. I read aloud for a few minutes. Then I repeated my first question: "What comes after your dialogue between southern and northern Brazil?"

Dom Helder picked up his pen and wrote:

"I am not an expert in economy. What I wish is that Brazilian enterprises will make an effort in the Northeast such as the United States made in postwar Europe with the Marshall Plan. In that case, the United States was moved by philanthropy, but also and above all, by intelligence. Who would be able to buy North American products if Western Europe were poor?"

There was no reason to believe that internal investment alone could solve the problem of misery and illiteracy in the Northeast, so I inserted a question: "Isn't a continental solution more realistic, opening up communications between all South American nations and developing the interior together?" I could hear Sergio Bernardes thundering, *"South America must become a continental nation!"*

Dom Helder smiled sadly as he wrote, "Surely you are correct. But unhappily, there is a certain absence of maturity here, a certain teen-age vanity that makes it almost impossible to establish a common Latin American market. And, of course, the Alliance for Progress is a factor. At this time, the Alliance is a well-meaning, but equivocal operation for the United States. You still do not pay just prices for the natural products of the Third World. For internal use, capitalism in the United States is twenty-first century capitalism. But for foreign use, it is nineteenth century capitalism. The position of the Soviet Union is the same— very selfish. You both take with the left hand what you give with the right.

"*Fidelismo*, for example, is the result of the want of understanding and sensibility on the part of the United States facing the struggle against underdevelopment and misery. And so is Catholic Marxism among Brazilian students. They are the creation of your anticommunism, which is unable to understand our hunger and thirst for justice. What we are facing is the want of

sensibility in our own privileged minority. I do not think Castro
was a communist until he was made desperate. And this same
thing could be repeated in each country in Latin America because always the extreme right is promoting anticommunism in
order to oppose economic development. When we do social work,
the extreme right says we are good. But when we promote development, we are called communists. I am not justifying. I am
understanding. The conditions in these underdeveloped countries
are inhuman. Thus, the biggest promoters of communism are the
extreme right, the extreme anticommunists. They do not understand the hunger for justice."

Dom Helder said his hand had grown weary. I took over as
stenographer. Then he read my next questions aloud and spoke
his answers looking over my shoulder as I wrote:

*"Is reform possible under present circumstances without a real
revolution?* When there is injustice, we need a real revolution in
the sense of total change. My friends tell me it is easier to raise up
the people through revolution than through reforming the structures. It is faster to open their eyes that way. I only say that if
you are opening their eyes and if the changes in structures are not
being done fast enough, you are preparing a revolution anyway.
For me, the current *situation* is revolutionary. The eyes of the
people will be opened with us or without us. If the latter, then
the Christian will be denounced as an ally of privilege. For me, it
is a human and Christian duty to open the eyes. Revolutionary is
the situation. I am not stating a position. I am stating reality.

"Can justice be achieved here within liberty? I like very much
the idea of liberty. But I have perhaps a contribution for my
North American friends whose dedication to the fight for liberty
is touching. I am always seeing young North Americans fighting
for liberty anywhere in the world each time it is endangered. But,
when one is born in a developed country, one does not have the
possibility for understanding that liberty is only a word for per-
sons without a house, without food, without a minimum of education, and without real work."

"Between rich and poor," I put in, plagiarizing Oscar Wilde, "the difference is that the poor always think about money." (The rest of it goes: *"That is the misery of being poor."*)

Dom Helder smiled bleakly and continued, which was a kind of acknowledgment. "Not only does communism crush liberty. Liberty is also crushed by inhuman conditions. The number one preoccupation is not to fight the communism, but to fight the underdevelopment. That is our duty. You see, here is the world divided between developed and underdeveloped. The developed countries are the white world, the civilized world, the ancient colonialist world, and the Christian world. Their manner of facing the underdeveloped world is with aid, but only in terms of no more than one per cent of the gross national product, and taking with the left hand the gift given with the right hand. Developed countries use words, words, words toward the Third World. It is only words to talk to a hungry man about communism. Justice would be to give each person not only aid, not only help, but to pay adequately for his products. That is why we need a general revision of the world market so that a group of privileged countries will not be the sole judges of prices. Justice is not possible, the underdeveloped countries cannot rise unless the international market is revised in terms of one world. Is this a dream? For me, Asia, Africa, and Latin America together represent a moral power without weapons. And it is only through moral power that there can be a revision of the international economic situation. I am denouncing the aid, the help, because it is not the solution. I know the answer of your government—that the unjust prices are the result of free trade. But a people is not only its government. A people is also its enterprises, its businessmen. I know this is a terrific political problem for America, but—development is the human, the Christian duty . . . Thus, there *can* be an end to anti-Americanism——"

Dom Helder stopped himself and took the pen from my hand to write:

"First must come understanding, friendship, mutual comprehension, and love. But second, until the people no longer see great monopolies (and for our people, monopolies are almost synonymous with the United States) taking the best of our natural resources, no aid, no help will touch our hearts." Dom Helder looked up at me. "St. Vincent explained that we must conquer by love the right of helping. You must understand this: It is terrible to receive."

His face cracked and he seemed about to weep.

Some minutes later, Dom Helder announced we must be off to the local TV station. Each week in Recife, he had taped two ten-minute programs, one for teen-agers and one for adults, called "We Are All Brothers." He also taped an occasional message for telecasting in Rio, his assignment for that afternoon. Dom Helder checked his pockets to be sure he carried his glasses, small whisk broom, soiled envelope containing a few thousand cruzeiros, and a mechanical toy "for the entertainment of the children." Then we walked down the steps, through the forbidding reception room, and across the palace yard to the street. Sunlight, diffused in moist clouds, changed all colors to gray-toned pastels. There was no breeze. My shirt stuck to my skin. Dom Helder, untroubled by the heat, flagged a taxi, whose driver kissed his hand. Then we drove off, down narrow streets, past a particularly glorious open air market with stalls full of green pineapples, yellow melons, purple-red tomatoes, and brown grain, to a commercial section not far from the edge of town. It was after three by the time we arrived at the studio, which was housed in a singularly grotesque example of Brazilian warehouse architecture. In the lobby, two carpenters embraced Dom Helder. The afternoon announcer embraced him, too. And the program director stood beside me, beaming as he waited his turn.

"In Brazil," he said proudly, "there are communists who hate the Church, but love Dom Helder."

After the *abraços*, we were rushed into a sound studio only to wait on a minor technical problem. Dom Helder, who was not one for small talk, took this opportunity to tell me about his maiden speech in Recife after his confrontation with Castelo Branco. He delivered it in April in the presence of two generals who had been ordered to monitor him for seditious nuances. "It was important to present my program," Dom Helder recalled, placing a finger to his lips and smiling conspiratorially. "So, those generals heard the speech of a pastor. I said I had no liaison with *any* group. I was pastor of all men because all men have the same Father. And when all men have the same Father, all men are brothers. I said that the house of the new archbishop would be open for all men, revolutionaries or not—I could say this aloud because, in Brazil, it is not easy to arrest a bishop—I also said we must not hate, for that creates bitterness. I said we must love. . . . You see, it is not easy for anyone to fight the position of love. That is how I feel. I am a Brazilian man, but always I have a universal preoccupation, more important than communism. Communism is a little problem, really. More important is the creation of a dialogue between the developed [he pointed north to America] and the developing [he pointed to the ground he stood on] nations. That is why I am massing public opinion through television, the press, and the transistor radio. If you are alone talking about development, you are called a communist. But if you get all the people together talking about it, everyone cannot be called a communist."

Then, as he stepped before the camera, Dom Helder gave himself a little Chaplinesque brush-up with his pocket whisk broom.

Half an hour later, with the sun dropping but still dangerous, Dom Helder took my arm and we walked to a bus stop. "I like to take the bus," he said, searching his white envelope for a small bill, "to be with the people." As we waited, a woman passing by stopped to ask Dom Helder about a school for her son. A man sought a blessing for his sick mother. And the driver of a small car crammed full of children offered him a lift back to the palacio. Then the bus came along, heading for Olinda, Recife's sister city of a hundred thousand people which had been one of Brazil's earliest Portuguese settlements. A youth gave Dom Helder his seat next to an old man who wore a tattered yachting cap, a grizzled beard, a shirt so often ripped that it had to be tied around his chest, ragged trousers, no shoes, and a pair of tiny spectacles through which he was reading the *Journal of Com-*

merce, Recife's leading daily newspaper. Dom Helder put on his glasses to read over the old man's shoulder. I stood in the aisle, looking out as the tropical landscape became, at once, more lush and humanly poorer. We passed a dreadful slum, perhaps fifty crude houses on low stilts over a bog. Anxiously, Dom Helder pulled my sleeve. "Do you see?" he asked.

The bus dropped us in the town square at Olinda where workmen were gilding a statue of a Romanesque figure holding a sledgehammer. Then we began a steep climb along a street of neat one-story yellow-and-pink houses. Magically, women and children appeared in almost every doorway to wave at the archbishop. He began to wilt as sweat rolled off his crown, but he gave a sign to everyone. At the top of the street there was a fine view of the ocean shore and to our right at the top of yet another knoll, the sixteenth-century Cathedral of Olinda. About fifty graduating architects along with their parents and sweethearts milled about in the front garden waiting for mass. I told Dom Helder that I would stay outside because I was unfamiliar with the service. "You must come in and enjoy it," he insisted. "It is for all men."

Moments later, he appeared in the sacristy transformed by a purple skull cap and splendid robes. He said the mass in Portuguese with grace and enthusiasm, and sometimes smiled as he prayed. The sermon (Dom Helder translated some of it for me later) suggested that his theme suited all occasions. "The architecture of Brazil is world famous," he said, "but it is only for the rich man. Now it must be for the poor . . . The poor are the Christ . . . A poor country does not need grand churches, it needs homes for the poor."

Afterwards, he left quickly, holding my arm as we started our descent to the town square. "Many architects," he said, "do not have faith in God, but like all artists, they participate in the power of the Divine. God loves all his children—Catholics, Protestants, Jews, and my friends, the artists."

Halfway down the hill, a stout, shabby man lay sprawled in the street. His hat and wine bottle lay ten feet away. Dom Helder ran to pick up the hat and kneel beside him. "Dío, dío, dío, dío," he said.

"Na, na, na," the man said.

"Here is your hat."

"Na, na, na."

Together, we lifted the man into a sitting position and propped him against a wall. His eyes were red and empty.

"Dío, dío, dío," Dom Helder chanted, as we hurried down the hill.

At dusk, we arrived in a grubby neighborhood near St. Peter's of Clergymen, the central cathedral of Recife. Narrow streets converging on the cathedral grounds were lined with tiny second-hand shops and overrun with sleazy dogs and cats. A chunk of meat frying over a fire in a cast-off oil drum did not seem to belong to anyone. For contrast, shiny cars inched ahead single-file toward the cathedral carrying dapper dons and their ladies, some in mink-trimmed evening wraps. The occasion was the society wedding of a newspaper publisher's daughter and a landlord's son. By the time we reached the door, the cream of Recife was pouring into the cathedral. I remarked on the chilly stares and cool greetings for Dom Helder as he was moving briskly toward a room behind the sacristy. Even the younger people seemed wary of him. "These people are very rich," Dom Helder said, "but I believe I must be the father of all the people."

I may have looked skeptical; in any case, as he changed robes, he explained further. "At least, you are seeing a typical day in my life, but there are times on an afternoon that I will meet as many as sixty or seventy poor supplicants at the palacio. To get through such an afternoon, I try to listen, look and speak as though I myself were the Christ. It is very tiring.

"I do have a certain ability to recoup my strength each night. I go to bed about eleven. Then precisely at two in the morning I stop dreaming and get out of bed. I pray and write for about two hours. Then I go back to sleep for an hour, awakening again at five to begin my day. It is that two A.M. prayer that rests my spirit. One can rest his spirit other ways—with nature, with art, with entertainment—but this is the best way for me. It is absolutely necessary to rest the spirit, because God would never consider giving grace to all men equally. That would be boring. He gives much grace to some and very little grace to others—and those, like myself, who have received much grace must be strong in order to give much in return to others. Therefore, I pray for all mankind, the rich and the poor, all of whose seven sins I have in myself."

The wedding did not last long and might have been over even sooner were it not for the relentless demands of four photographers and an assistant carrying a bank of flood lights.

Afterwards, Dom Helder hurried to make his getaway. He went unnoticed in the throng. Shortly, we returned to the palacio for a quick meal of soup, rice, meat, potatoes, and tropical yams. Then Dom Helder announced we would leave at 7:30 P.M. for the high school graduation to return in time for an appearance at the reception for David Bell and Lincoln Gordon in a downtown auditorium. The reception had been planned as a more or less public affair following a V.I.P. dinner for which Dom Helder had an invitation. He told me the invitation had arrived after he had agreed to appear at the high school, so he could only attend the public reception.

As it turned out, the high school was ninety minutes by car from Recife over broken roads, past three carnivals, and down several wrong turnings to a remote suburb. Even before we arrived, I knew we would never get back in time to honor the American aid program. I thought Dom Helder, a man who understood symbolism, had known this all along. In the high school auditorium, he asked me to join him on the narrow stage along with a dozen local dignitaries. From there, we looked out over an audience that did not quite fill the room. Many graduates had stayed away, Dom Helder told me, because they were unable to afford the necessary blue suit or party dress. Thus, each non-answer to a name on the list of graduates was followed by a pitiful silence. But, the ceremony was touching and not really interminable. Each youth came forward alone, accepted a scroll, and was congratulated by the adults on the stage, myself included. Then he or she returned to the audience where his or her sweetheart nervously waited with a kiss. These kisses landed on the forehead, nose, ears, neck or teeth but rarely on the lips. Then, to thunderous applause, the parents embraced both children and all four sat down, usually weeping. All this was repeated about forty times. Then came the valedictorian's unedited, thirty-minute panegyric on the responsibilities of modern youth. After that, there were additional comments by each celebrity on the stage, myself excluded. At times, the archbishop slept. But he was awake when, as the speeches droned on, a church bell somewhere struck ten. Leaning close to me, he said: "Too bad I will never be able to make the reception for your David Bell . . . I will miss seeing Ambassador Lincoln Gordon. He is a good and wonderful man."

Dom Helder interrupted himself to applaud the end of a particularly solemn speech. Then, during a respite before the next one, he continued: "But you know, it is not *aid* we want from America. It is justice. We don't want *help*, we want justice. Did you know that your aid does not even equal your *gain* from our losses due to the deflation of Brazilian commodity prices in your market?"

Next day Dom Helder flew to Rio for a week of social work conferences. I might have saved myself the trip to Recife, but then I would have missed the plane ride with him that morning.

Early on, I packed my bag and ate a good breakfast of mangos and flapjacks. With the help of a bilingual waiter, I also read a *Journal of Commerce* article by Calazans Fernandes about *Terceiro Mundo*, the Third World. Senhor Fernandes, inspired by the reception for David Bell, wrote as Dom Helder had talked. Why, he asked, does the United States foreign aid amount to less than the aid of France, less than one percent of its gross national product for development in the Third World?

At nine A.M., Dom Helder and the old nun met me at the airport. She urged me to take good care of him. I said I would try. When we boarded our flight, Dom Helder turned and waved a Kleenex at her. She waved a scarf and both dabbed at their eyes. It was unlikely, however, that she feared for his safety. Once while flying on a plane with a defective landing gear, Dom Helder had been asked by the pilot to pray for a safe touchdown. He prayed, and the plane landed without incident—until just after the last crew member debarked. Then the landing gear collapsed. I had heard this story from three sources and Dom Helder admitted that something like it had indeed happened. Many people believed God had a special interest in him.

For the flight to Rio, Dom Helder chose a center seat among three seats abreast in the tourist section. I sat on the aisle. And a rough-looking Brazilian, about fifty with a mashed nose and a purple face, sat by the window on Dom Helder's right. The tough wore a sky-blue suit and a matching (except for grease spots) sweater. Between his knees, he held a quart-jug of red wine. Grandly, while we fastened our safety belts, he presented his calling card. His name was *Valentine Glimberg*. His title identified him as a petty official in the agriculture secretariat, Rio branch. Dom Helder shook Glimberg's hand, I shook it, and then Glimberg lapsed into a reverie, repeating our names over and over, drooling purple wine over his purple chin.

We flew south above thick clouds with only an occasional glimpse of the gray ocean below. Dom Helder had brought the *Journal of Commerce* with him. He re-read part of the Fernandes article and said Fernandes' point was well-taken. "If you buy my products at an unjust price, I have the right of crying," Dom Helder said. "You, of course, decide whether or not to give your development aid. This year it comes to about one dollar per person in Latin America. But the point is that it is not justice. You see, more important than your money is your *comprehension* . . . For example, it is my view that the Castelo Branco revolution was not a real revolution. True, we had read in the press about certain evils under Goulart. A certain infiltration of communism. A certain irresponsibility from the President. A certain mistake in handling money. But, as Goulart was always talking about reforming structures, the economic interests of the south used radio, press, and television to make you and the world think Brazil was beginning a new Cuba. And the Army was *sure* that this was true. This I understand. Even though the evils were very, very exaggerated, they *were* real.

"But the situation was really very different from Castro's Cuba. We were told about the preparation of a Cubanistic combination between certain workers and certain members of the Army—this was not true. If it had been true, Castelo Branco and the Army could not take over, *completely*, in less than two days. But they did, so fast that they had no program, no preparation . . . Now, I myself told the new President that the word *revolution* is a sacred name and should not be used for just an anti-communist government. The only hope for justice is through reform, I told him. It is an illusion that you can arrest a few communists and the trouble is over. Now see what has happened. When Castelo Branco called in a few advisers to make a plan, he himself was called a communist by the economic powers. The result is that we have a new government with great contradictions. On the one hand, they say they want to reform structures, but on the other hand, they have a planning minister unable to understand development. They believe the only way to fight inflation is to develop our south more and make it richer. This, of course, will only delay the inevitable."

Halfway to Rio, our neighbor, Valentine Glimberg, finished his wine. He had been listening to Dom Helder and humming along with the music piped into our cabin. At the moment, the tune was *Blues in the Night.* Valentine belched.

"You are right, dear father!" he said, in thickly accented English. "It is impossible to stop Brazil." He exhaled wine fumes into Dom Helder's ear while clapping a hand on his shoulder. "They cannot stop Brazil!"

Dom Helder smiled lovingly. "You are a good friend," he said. "You like the Church as I am seeing it."

Valentine looked fiercely at me. "I like American people," he exclaimed. "I no like American's government! America is racist! I tell you, young man—Morgan—God is not a white man!"

In furious Portuguese, Valentine described an experience he had once had in New York. Dom Helder translated for me: "Senhor Glimberg says he and a Negro friend could not get a room together in a New York hotel."

"Right!" Valentine growled. Then he snatched a glass of beer from the tray of a passing steward. "Ha!" he cried, sloshing foam on Dom Helder's cassock. He switched the glass from left to right hand. Then he flung his free arm around Dom Helder's neck.

Bom Dom!" he shouted. "Good Bishop! I'm sorry!"

Unperturbed, Dom Helder freed himself and smiled at me. "We have segregation in Brazil, too," he said. "We have very real economic segregation. We have no Negro bishops, no Negro architects, no Negro engineers. Negroes have no economic opportunity. Until 1888, we had slavery, so practically all of our Negroes are the descendants of slaves. It has not been easy for them to rise. In America—I have been there several times—I have often seen Negroes driving big cars. Negroes can become rich men in America. But in Brazil, there is economic segregation. It is not forbidden for the Negro to rise, but he does not rise."

Valentine Glimberg listened with a kind of leaden intensity. "Ho, *amigo!*" he shouted to me. "I love you."

Then once again he spoke furious Portuguese.

" 'God is just!' " Dom Helder said Valentine had said. " 'And because He is just, He will destroy America like He destroyed Sodom and Gomorrah. America is all propaganda and confusion. Korea! Vietnam! The burning of churches! Even Russia does not burn churches! America is dominated by six families!' "

Dom Helder translated with feeling. But he suddenly seemed tired of the exchange and shrank fromValentine's next grappling *abraço*.

"Dom Helder is cardinal of the people!" Valentine cried, again spilling beer on the archbishop's cassock.

They both laughed; it was nothing.

"I like American coffee," Valentine insisted. "I like American beds. American *love*." (Pronounced *lawvf.*)

At this point, Dom Helder excused himself and retreated to the lavatory.

"Where you from, *amigo?*" Valentine asked.

"New York," I said.

"Papa?"

"Illinois."

"Grandpapa?"

"Crimea."

"Russia! Russia!" Valentine shook my hand. "I knew I like you. Every American from Russia is Yiddish. You Yiddish?"

"Yes."

"Aha! I like you. I Yiddish, too. Karl Marx is Yiddish. Trotsky is Yiddish. Einstein is Yiddish. Me, I am a communist. Yes, I am a Trotskyite communist. Ho! I no like the American Yiddish." Valentine pounded his fist on Dom Helder's empty seat. "But you and me, we are blood brothers. King Solomon. King David. Christos. St. Paul. All Yiddish! Catholics, *fooey!*"

He dismissed Dom Helder with a back-of-the-hand motion. Then, as though he had been slugged, Valentine Glimberg fell asleep.

In time, Dom Helder returned and we prepared for the landing at Rio. "You know that Rio is not my home," he said. "I was born in the little town of Fortaleza in Ceará. There were fifteen in my family. My father was a bookkeeper and my mother taught primary school. My father was not a religious man, but I always wanted to be a priest. He asked me once if I knew what it meant to be a priest. I asked him to tell me. So, this man of no religion, my father, presented me a picture of the priesthood:

"'A priest,' my father said, 'is a man unable to be selfish. He must live for others. He has no right to seek money. He is a man for the people and for God.'

"And I answered, 'I want to be a priest now more than ever.'

"So, my father blessed me. Then I went to the seminary in Fortaleza and became a priest in 1931. I went to work among the teachers and workers and at twenty-five, became the government's director of education in the town. I was a specialist in education and was invited to come to Rio in 1936. Over the years, the *favelas* grew out of inhuman conditions in the rural zones. I knew that the solution to the *favelas* was very complex, but I was certain the Church itself must be present in them. So, in the 1950's we began the work to help the *favelados*. This brought me to the heart of the development issue. I saw that in Brazil itself we have both developed and underdeveloped regions. Brazil *is* the world, so it is important to understand her. Yes, it is important even for the North Americans."

Our plane rolled to a stop in front of the main arrival building.

Valentine Glimberg awoke singing the Marseillaise. "How come you Americans never speak any other language, eh, *amigo?*" he demanded.

"I speak Yiddish," I said. At that Valentine yelled happily and crushed Dom Helder and me together in his powerful arms.

On the ramp outside, about one hundred women and eight Boy Scouts flocked around to welcome Dom Helder. Most of the women were associates in his on-going welfare programs in Rio. There were television cameramen on hand, too, as well as several reporters who had been alerted by Dom Helder's boosters, mindful of publicity values. As we emerged, the Boy Scouts stamped to attention. One blew a whistle and the others shouted a three-cheer salute. Dom Helder flashed his round-eyed smile and was immediately swamped by an all-embracing, finger-kissing, back-slapping, cassock-clutching horde, duly filmed for the evening news. Like some super-centipede, the crowd moved *en masse* into the terminal. I thought I had lost Dom Helder, but his hand emerged above the throng and then his voice, assuring me that he would see me to my hotel.

On the way, with one of the ladies at the wheel of a Simca, we saw earth-moving machines and cement mixers and men working on the landscape along miles of new parkways. Every few hundred yards, a sign credited Governor Carlos Lacerda for the road beautification program. Dom Helder said he felt Lacerda was an immature man, but could become President someday if Castelo Branco permitted free elections. Passing through the central business district, I saw a boy dodging through a traffic jam carrying a stack of telephone books on his head. Nearing the beach, Dom Helder pointed out an exotic outdoor shrine with hundreds of white candles burning on its steps. On the wall behind, someone had painted "Viva Goulart!" and someone else had all but painted it out.

At last, there was Copacabana, a golden strip of incongruity, spotted with umbrellas and embroidered by a serpentine mosaic walk, along which a lone, memorable long-haired girl happened to be jiggling.

I said *adiós* to Dom Helder and, a few days later, took off for Japan.

3
Japanese

Christmas eve, in the midst of the Japanese New Year celebration, I moved into a hotel in Tokyo. When I checked out three weeks later, the celebration was still going on, with no end in sight. People did not seem to know when it would end—only that it had begun with the winter solstice. I liked their attitude.

If I could adapt one Japanese tradition to American life, it would be this open-ended holiday, full of contagious delights, dances, festivals, and prodigious love-making. At New Year's, the Japanese are more *Japanese* than at other times of the year or, rather, less occidental. They expect women to put away their Western clothes for the duration and wear kimonos and sandals in public. Having cultivated privacy all year long, even more assiduously than their gardens, they open their homes to friends and venture out to call on their neighbors. They settle the year's accounts, paying in cash (no one writes checks) and receiving in return a gift of soap or saki or some other useful item from smiling shopkeepers. They even visit Shinto shrines to pray for good luck just in case there are gods who still care. And, above all, they slow down, which is supremely out of character for the hustling Japanese. People I met were always apologizing for their holiday mood and inviting me to return when things were really moving.

There were contradictions. The weather, ushering in 1965, the Year of the Snake, was cold and indifferent. Snow fell every other day. Nights were damp. And the sun, at its best, gave off a melancholy light. The thinnest man in the world grimly pulled an enclosed rickshaw on the Ginza, the Broadway of Tokyo; the postwar regulations prohibiting *man*powered vehicles exempted him because he had a geisha girl inside. An old woman shuffled through an arcade with logs on her back. And a panhandler warmed his hands over a fire in the alley behind the Imperial Hotel. But the New Year's spirit prevailed. Holiday lanterns hung from the sky. Bells rang at random. And besides the girls in their costumes, happy drunks brightened the streets on their way home from company parties. We Japanese had a fine time.

The new power of Japan seemed to astonish everyone I met and Tokyo was its symbol. Sixty per cent destroyed during World War II, the city is up again—an ugly, neon brute dominated by new-minted skyscrapers, pierced by the screams of streamliners, and choked in traffic. All lines of influence converge here. The system in Japan is braced by traditions of discipline and status, and substantiated by prosperity. It is managed by an elite whose Prime Minister is, in effect, the nation's top businessman. Government is business and business is government, maintained and enhanced by strategically arranged marriages. Family means power, derived from the foresight of the first postwar cabinet whose members helped rebuild the economy and then turned it over to their relatives in the *samurai* class. In exchange for U.S. military bases, we not only insured Japan's security but also its growth. We could not, however, provide an effective, flexible opposition for the ruling Liberal-Democrats. The Japanese left has been a collection of manageable factions, split on foreign as well as domestic issues; the right has been vastly outnumbered. As a result, many Japanese frustrated by the status quo are uninspired by its conventional critics. They feel a need to belong to a militant *something*. Thus, scores of new Buddhist sects are flourishing, especially Sokagakkai, which claims an enthusiastic membership of five million and has created Komeito, a "clean government" political party beginning to elect its members to the Diet. In the coming fight over renewal of the United States-Japan mutual security pact, which expires in 1970, Komeito might emerge as the Liberal-Democrat's most meaningful competitor. For what it's worth, the names of Japan's best-selling cigarettes are *Hope, Peace,* and *Harmony.*

The morning after Christmas, Dr. Shigeto Tsuru, a professor of economics at Hitotsubashi University, who has had a substantial following among socialist intellectuals (a virtual redundancy in Japan), came to fetch me at my hotel—a gesture of courtesy quite routine for him, but unique and touching for me, having spent much of my workaday life calling on others. I had telephoned him and he had said he would take me to lunch and then to his club where I might question him at length. He was a pleasantly brisk man in his early fifties, short and stocky with a determined chin and the inevitable glasses. He wore a somber gray suit with a vest, black tie, and starched collar. "I want you to try one of my favorite restaurants," he said, and we set off along the Ginza amid crowds of holiday shoppers.

The street swarmed with cars and bikes and daredevil pedestrians. Store windows bulged with stylish clothes, shoes, tools, cutlery, pens, cameras, gongs, toys and, of course, all sorts of miniature electronic devices. There were no empty stores, no wasted spaces, and the geometry of new construction loomed overhead. Tsuru explained that he himself did not often come into the central shopping district. He was living in a residential section of town as far from the Ginza as Wall Street is from midtown Manhattan. Each day he traveled an hour by commuter train to his university in the suburbs.

By and by, we came to a tiny, well-scrubbed cafe specializing in raw seafood and strange vegetables wrapped around hand-rolled balls of cold rice—*sushi.* Tsuru ordered for me and seemed relieved that I enjoyed my meal. He lamented the passing of the sushi tradition in Japan. It seems that masters of the art of slicing and serving raw octupi, eels, and various exotic fish are growing old, while apprentices are increasingly hard to find as impatient young men seek more promising work in industry.

"It takes time to become a sushi-master," Tsuru said, "especially, to learn how to roll the rice. An apprentice may not even hold the rice until he has accomplished all other phases of the art."

Since much had been written about the postwar emancipation of Japanese women, I asked if it were possible to bring them into the sushi trade. With appropriate seriousness, Tsuru replied that there could be *no* female sushi-masters.

"Women's hands are too warm for the rice," he said.

After lunch, in a taxi heading for the University Club, we passed the Imperial Palace, a foreboding castle amid evergreen gardens on a fortress island surrounded by a moat virtually in the center of town. Tsuru told me that the daily press had been reporting the holiday activities of the Emperor with more detail than usual this season. There were many explanations for this phenomenon, coming after twenty years of imperial de-emphasis, but Tsuru felt the most likely one was economic. Japan was a going concern, operating in the black (World War II had wiped out her debt) on the basis of short-term loans from its best customer, the United States. But a scarcity of manpower had developed in recent months, followed by inflation. This had squeezed many small businessmen and contributed to a sharp rise in business failures, which in turn created general economic tension—and a need for diversions like Emperor "worship." Presumably, if the labor supply would catch up with the demand, the press would pay less attention to the Emperor. I had no way to verify Tsuru's theory, but there was no doubt that he meant what he said. He had a fine, sharp mind, seemingly unburdened by a sense of humor.

Tsuru and I spent most of the afternoon seated at a table in the University Club restaurant, a staid, quiet retreat overlooking a precise inner garden. Except for the waiter, who periodically filled our teacups and emptied our ashtray, no one approached us. In this time, Tsuru told me the story of his life.

He was born in the city of Nagoya, the son of a civil engineer who later worked as an executive of the local gas company. In 1929, at age seventeen, he had entered the "higher school," or gymnasium. Japanese troops were already fighting in China and military training was required of the gymnasium boys. Tsuru opposed both and soon joined a student protest movement, which gave him "the opportunity to study socialism" in reading societies sponsored by the movement. "Of course," Tsuru recalled, "the school administration prohibited the study of Karl Marx and the Soviet Union, so we met in secret hiding places and published weekly mimeographed papers about what was going on in Russia. We associated ourselves with similar movements in other universities and also with the outlawed trade-union movement. The atmosphere was such that it took courage to stand for our motto: *Hands off China*. The police were always picking up our newspaper. But out of eight hundred students at my school, we were able to influence nearly two hundred. We became so strong that we were able to upset the next semi-annual military drill and maneuvers. When the final drill-command for attack was given, we threw down our guns.

"Soon after this, December 2, 1930, thirty-six of us were arrested. The police had followed our activities and knew I was one of the top ring leaders. So, while thirty-three of the boys were released in a week, three of us were kept in jail for three months while the police made investigations. Finally, I was prosecuted, sentenced, put on probation, and released. Then, when I returned to school, I found I had been expelled under a regulation forbidding an unreported absence of more than thirty days. My name was expunged from all records which meant I could go to no other public school in Japan."

Tsuru next had resolved to go to school in a foreign country. And like most Japanese students going abroad in 1931, he preferred Germany. "I wanted to go there to continue my study of Karl Marx," Tsuru said. "But my father was sure I would soon be in the same kind of trouble as before and said he would only help me if I went to the United States. So, I agreed. But I intended to wait only a year or two and then go secretly to Germany. He gave me $2500—5,000 yen at that time—and told me to try to be an independent man."

Tsuru chose Lawrence College in Appleton, Wisconsin, an inexpensive school with no other Japanese students on the campus. "I lied to get in," he admitted, "telling the president I had already finished higher school in Nagoya."

Entering as a freshman in September, 1931, Tsuru plotted to leave for Germany in 1933. But the longer he remained at Lawrence, the more he thought about staying. He worked as a waiter and ran for the cross-country team. Among the faculty, he got to know Harry Dexter White, who was teaching a Marxist history of economics, and Gordon Clapp, the freshman dean, who later became director of T.V.A. "It was Gordon Clapp more than anyone else who made me learn about the United States and appreciate it. I decided to stay, to really study America, and asked Gordon what I should do. After two years at Lawrence, he urged me to go to Harvard. My father sent more money, so I transferred."

In 1935, Tsuru graduated from Harvard, *magna cum laude,* and was elected to Phi Beta Kappa. The following year, he won a Master's Degree. Then he became a faculty assistant, which paid him enough to continue his studies for a Ph.D. under J. A. Schumpeter. Among his friends at the time were two other young economists, Paul Samuelson and Robert Triffin. And he often attended Sunday teas at the home of Arthur Schlesinger, Sr.

While working on his dissertation, applying the theory of business cycles to Japan, Tsuru wrote home, asking his father and eldest sister to collect photographs of eligible maidens. He wanted a wife. "I judged the photographs on my next visit to Nagoya," Tsuru said. "I selected one girl's picture and then I met the girl. In an arranged marriage, after this first meeting, either side can ease itself out or indicate a desire to meet again. We met again. Then, through a go-between, I made a proposal. And after a respectable time had passed, her father replied. He was a scientist, director of the Institute of Aeronautical Studies at Tokyo University. His older brother was the Emperor's chief political adviser—after the war, he was arrested as a war criminal, served a time in prison, and is now free. . . . Anyway, the reply came back: 'We are happy to give our daughter to you.' "

Married in 1939 and awarded his doctorate at Harvard in 1940, Tsuru had returned home to hunt for a teaching job. But then, as now, the academic establishment looked upon a returning scholar as an outsider. "Our society respects a man who comes from his own university," Tsuru said. "One is expected to start from the beginning at, say, Tokyo University in order to get a job later—at Tokyo University. Thus, I could only go back to Harvard. I was in Cambridge when the war started and had to register as an enemy alien. The authorities asked me to hand in my camera and report whenever I wished to move more than thirty miles outside Cambridge. But otherwise, my wife and I were not treated badly. Then, although Harvard asked me to stay on in the department of economics, we came back on the first exchange boat and I became a diplomat. That was 1942, and I was just thirty years old. During the war, I served in China and the Soviet Union as well as Tokyo. My house was never bombed."

In the early years of the occupation, Tsuru worked in an economic research unit. Later he was vice-minister of economic stabilization under the ten-month administration of Prime Minister Kotayama, a Socialist. Then, in 1948, with the Liberal-Democrats firmly in power and the Japanese "American revolution" progressing apace, Tsuru joined the Institute for Economic Research at Hitotsubashi University. He directed the Institute until 1956. Then under an exchange program jointly sponsored by the Rockefeller Foundation and International House of Japan, he returned to Harvard as a visiting professor and, early the following year, received a subpoena from the Senate Internal Security Committee.

Tsuru said he could have ignored the subpoena, but he had felt that it was better to testify than to leave oneself open for a subsequent F.B.I. investigation. "My name got to them like this: If you will read the records of the McCarthy committee, you will find that the Institute of Pacific Relations had a managing director who stored all the memos, letters, and documents he had ever received—in a barn in Connecticut. Interested in the activities of the Institute, the F.B.I. had retrieved this data and investigated it. My name appeared in a number of memos in connection with research projects and plans of the Institute. Moreover, my name pretty certainly had connections with all kinds of things in other F.B.I. files. And my wife's name appeared in a political connection because another one of her relatives is a permanent unofficial Japanese representative in Peking.

"Now, in March, 1957, the Senate committee also became interested in the Canadian ambassador to Cairo, E. H. Norman. At this time, the Middle-Eastern situation was tense and there was feeling that the Canadian ambassador was not cooperating with United States policy. Looking into Norman, the Senate committee found that he had left-wing associations in the United States. And during the questioning of a member of the State Department, my name was mentioned. Pretty certainly, the committee had read the F.B.I.'s files on me. And when the fact that I knew Norman came out, it became inevitable that I should be asked to appear. I discussed the matter with J. K. Galbraith, who urged me to go and use candor, the best kind of weapon. So I went to Washington thinking I would be questioned about Norman. They asked me about him—and more. I was amazed at the extent of my material they had. Even letters I had written! I was asked about my activities and associations in the United States during the Thirties. I was asked about my activities in postwar Japan and my associations with Americans in the Occupation suspected of being left-wing. They made public my connection with the left-wing magazine, *Science and Society*, started in the United States in 1936. I had helped plan it. And they also publicized the fact that I had organized and participated in discussion groups to study Karl Marx in the same period when there was a natural interest in social criticism of capitalism.

"After my hearing, the Boston *Herald* wrote an editorial saying it had all been impolite, that it was not nice to subject a foreign visitor to such questioning. Galbraith and others wrote a letter to the New York *Times* criticizing the committee. But to me, it was not an especially important incident. It gave me an insight into the functions of that kind of committee, but it did not change my attitude toward the United States. Nor did it leave an especially important imprint on my career. It was simply an unpleasant and unnecessary episode. But there was a tremendous reaction in Japan, pro and con. The Senate committee was denounced and so was I. Then it all faded and, in 1960, I returned to America. I stayed almost two years, lecturing at Yale, Johns Hopkins, the University of Rochester, New York University, the University of Minnesota, and Harvard. Now I have just returned from a tour of Australia as a Dyason Memorial lecturer following, among others, Gunnar Myrdal, Bertrand Russell, and Arnold Toynbee. . . ."

Tsuru interrupted his story at this point. The afternoon was gone. I suggested we meet again on the following day. Tsuru shook his head, showing me that the day had been crossed off in his date-book. He said he must help his wife clean the house and cook for the holidays. "We live 'Japanese' at home," he said. "I wear a kimono, keep a perfect garden, and attend to rituals. At New Year's time, there are five days when we do no work, so we must clean and look ahead. This is my Japanese double life. Outwardly, the Japanese imitate the West. In private, we maintain our national culture . . . I might say that we are now beginning to criticize this dichotomy between public ugliness and private beauty. Foreigners, for example, rarely come into contact with our private life. We don't invite guests to our homes, but to a restaurant like this—and usually stag. All this has cost us dearly. We have lost the creativity that flourished in feudal Japan. But now we are thinking about external harmony and beauty again. I think we are on the threshold of harmonizing the old and the new, the East and the West. Before you leave Tokyo, you must visit me in my home."

Tsuru smiled warmly for the first time.

"This dichotomy is very important to understand," he said. "In the past one hundred years, Japan has produced nothing of significance in our cultural fields, no ideas, no novels, no philosophy. With some exceptions, this is the price of a double life, of being Westernized."

At my hotel next afternoon, Akira Kuroyanagi, "Chief of the General Overseas Bureau of Sokagakkai," picked me up in a black sedan. He was a stout, bluff fanatic, about thirty-two, with a whispering, passionate voice. He always spoke as though making a speech, but quietly. Akira and his brother had once belonged to the Communist Party. In 1951, at the time of the riots protesting the war in Korea, the Bomb, and the Occupation, his brother was killed in a scuffle. Then their mother developed cancer. She joined Sokagakkai, which was just then emerging out of the spiritual interpretations of a few Buddhists, and was cured. This miracle, following the senseless death of his brother, led Akira away from communism and into Sokagakkai, but not all at one jump. He estimated that it took him two years to master *Philosophy of Value* and other basic works on righteous living by Tsunesaburo Makiguchi, first president of Sokagakkai. Makiguchi had died in 1944 in Sugamo Prison after his conviction for blasphemy against the Emperor. Sokagakkai changed Akira's life. He had been poor, he said, and now he was a little rich. Besides handling foreign press relations, he edited Sokagakkai's weekly papers, three monthly journals, and assorted pamphlets published in five languages. Moreover, Sokagakkai gave him personal pride. He boasted that one hundred thousand families per month were joining up. He predicted that Komeito would be Japan's second-largest political party by 1967 and the majority party by 1969. "It is destined," he would say.

After a long drive through Tokyo, Akira parked the car and guided me toward Nihonu Auditorium, a domed stadium where samurai wrestlers used to fight. The time was precisely 4:30 P.M. Presumably, Akira was under orders not to arrive a minute too soon—or until twenty thousand neatly and modestly dressed men and women, young and old, some with babes in arms, had filled every seat, every inch of standing room in the auditorium. I was to feel the full impact of their numbers, and I did. They jammed the auditorium floor with eager bodies and rapt eyes hungering toward one hundred and fifty men in black suits with white shirts and dark ties sitting on an unadorned stage. They also filled three tiers of encircling balconies, only allowing space for a brass band and a girls' fife-and-drum corps in golden uniforms. The moment we arrived they were singing the *Caisson Song*. Then the music stopped. On the stage, a stupefyingly serious leader removed his jacket, unfolded a golden fan, and with sharp, cutting gestures conducted that great crowd *a cappella* in the Sokagakkai song—to the effect that "a new epoch" had begun and that "the propagation of Sokagakkai" would go on all over the world. Over a disciplined explosion of applause, Akira said, "Welcome to the monthly meeting for this area."

After the song, a second leader spoke briefly into a microphone. Then a third picked up the golden fan and led the Sokagakkai song once more. A fourth man talked, the fifth conducted—again the song. The meeting went on like this for an hour, the song rising each time in ever-increasing ecstasy. At last, Daisaku Ikeda, third and current president of Sokagakkai, stepped to the microphone. From a distance, he looked young and strong. Akira said Ikeda was not yet forty. And laughing confidentially, he said he was no relation to the former prime minister. Ikeda had prepared a *haiku* poem for the occasion. As he began to read, twenty thousand people groped for twenty thousand pencils and took dictation. Then, Ikeda removed *his* coat. With his right hand on his hip and the golden fan held high in his left, he led the song three times over, building the sound to the dome and trying to push it through.

Afterwards, Akira promised he would try to arrange a meeting with Ikeda for me, but he said I should not feel optimistic.

"American correspondents," Akira said, "have insultingly referred to the way he leads our song as 'Ikeda's fan dance.' "

"They're not serious," I said.

"We don't understand your sense of humor. . . ."

Tsuru came to my hotel again the next day. He removed his coat and sat by the window, ready to go on with his story. I served tea as best I could. Then I sat on my bed to listen.

"Before the war," he said, "I was probably more radical than in the postwar period. I think you can explain this in terms of the Japanese domestic scene. Anyone opposed to the military prewar had to be united in radicalism. There was no differentiation between communists and socialists then. We were all Marxists. I never belonged to the Communist Party or to the Young Communist League, but you could identify me as a Marxist intellectual."

I wondered what had restrained him from joining the party. Tsuru explained, or tried, using the labels of his generation.

"I had learned in America a great deal about pragmatism by studying James and Dewey. Gradually, then, I lost interest in the doctrine of Marx and became critical of both doctrinaire Marxism and investigations of 'what Marx meant.' I became more practical and pragmatic and, although I did not join, I became identified with the Socialist Party. Today, I belong to the left side of the Socialist Party. Yet among two thousand Japanese economists, I stand slightly to the right of center. Do you understand? I am a left-wing socialist politically and ideologically, but we have so many hard-boiled orthodox Marxist economists, I am considered to the right of center among them. Anyway, our situation is changing. The doctrinaire Marxists are fading away. More and more are being attracted to Keynes and Schumpeter, to econometrics and practicality. In ten years, those who are only interested in Marxist text interpretations will be a small minority."

"What's the difference now between a Socialist and a Liberal-Democrat?" I asked, expecting more labels. But Tsuru instinctively associated the question with Japanese self-interest.

"In foreign policy, the major issue is the defense of Japan," he said. "The Liberal-Democrats think more or less like the United States' State Department. They consider the Chinese communists a threat to the peace and security of this area. We Socialists do not think the Chinese communists are a threat to us. Socialist policy, therefore, says 'recognize China, admit China to the United Nations, enlarge trade with China, and look at Formosa as an internal Chinese problem' . . . I personally do not feel that the communist Chinese are a threat to Southeast Asia. If, for example, the Vietnamese people do not solve their problems, the communists within may take over through indirect invasion. But you see, the question is not what one is against, but what one is for. One must answer this question. There are intrinsic difficulties in places like Vietnam, and the wisest man probably could not have done better than the Americans. But the orientation of Mr. Dulles was much too anticommunist. And it happened that land reform specialists in America were progressives and socialists. Your best man, Wolf Ladijinsky, was under a McCarthy cloud. Thus, you did not push land reform and your Mekong delta proposals have come very, very late in the day."

Listening to Tsuru, I was intrigued by his tactic of prefacing a harsh criticism with gentle praise. We were "wise" but we had been stupid. I smiled and he smiled, apparently assuming that my feelings were hurt.

"I respect your belief against communism," he continued. "But you have let it tie your hands. You have failed to put enough emphasis on positive programs in Vietnam and in Thailand and elsewhere. Very late, you have tried to shift your emphasis, but this is difficult. The point *I* want to emphasize is this: The manner in which Americans have seen the problems of the world are too political and not sufficiently economic. But even as weapons keep on improving, a *modus vivendi* between America and Russia is on the way. The knotty problem is China. I do not know how you will decide about this . . . Perhaps when we solve the problem in Vietnam, one way or another, the air will clear. It may be that America will have an isolationist reaction if Vietnam turns out to be a debacle. You may even decide that it is not for America to deal at all with certain parts of the world . . . It is a key fact that we can never be sure that America will always want to involve herself everywhere in the world. . . ."

There was a tall, delicate ex-showgirl named Taeko Kato whom I often visited in the tiny cafe she managed on a back street in Akasaka, one of the nightlife districts of Tokyo. She was about thirty and liked to be called "Momma-san." After my first visit, she always kissed me when I walked in. It would be useless to speculate on what that kiss meant to her. I liked Taeko very much. And her cafe, called Oyuki. Oyuki consisted of a counter with eight stools, two small tables and a booth. Behind the counter, a girl named Ami, who had once studied interior decorating at New York University, served dainty meals, saki, mixed drinks, and tea. Ami also operated the record player. At this season, her favorite number was *Rudolph, the Red-Nosed Reindeer,* sung in Japanese. A glass case on the counter displayed the selection of raw fish and vegetables offered on the menu. Bamboo scrolls, devil masks, and drawings from ancient myths decorated the walls. Paper lanterns dangled from the ceiling. The effect was somehow magical and had the power to transform a banal assortment of customers, mostly quiet young Japanese men, junior executives and medical students, rebellious shopgirls, prostitutes, and strays from the foreign correspondents' press club into romantic and mysterious wayfarers of the Orient. One night, a Swiss journalist came in, just back from Peking and a journey down the Yangtze. He said the communists' triumph in China was *simply* the organization of six hundred million people to feed and clothe themselves. Another regular was the son of an attaché at one of the embassies. He had been studying Karate and bragged he would soon depart for Israel to teach it at the Weizmann Institute.

Taeko Kato was everybody's friend. Mostly, she stared into your face and listened to you talk. But if you became too rational, she would bat her lashes, back away, and dance with herself. I had complained about the music and wound up donating a Miles Davis album to Ami's small record library. Taeko often danced to Miles' solos.

You were welcome to sit for hours at Oyuki over a cup of a tea or a single pitcher of saki. Taeko would light your cigarettes, rub your back, wipe your face with a cool towel, and button your overcoat when it was time to go. She would clean your glasses if you gave her a chance. Now and then, she made a bawdy joke about you—or about Janko, the girl in the lace dress and heavy eye-shadow who usually sat at one end of the counter waiting for telephone calls. If the telephone rang, Janko might disappear for an hour or two. But if you stayed late, she always returned. Occasionally, I stayed very late at Oyuki and played cards with Janko.

One night, Taeko came in with a set of ladies' golf clubs wrapped in cellophane and tied with a holiday ribbon. She said it was a present from an admirer. Then she knocked a hole in a lantern swinging the driver.

Taeko told me she had several current admirers, but no true lover since the last one, whom she had rejected that summer. "Warm heart," she said, "but he had no brains." She asked me to understand that she could not support a brainless boyfriend as well as her mother and father on the profits of a small cafe. Besides, she was in no mood for love. The recent death of the film actor, Oyuki, who had financed her business, had broken her heart, perhaps forever. Taeko, under the rice powder and red, red lipstick, always looked tragic when she spoke of Oyuki.

Taeko taught me that "Westernized" was a precarious label for modern Japan, despite our usual assumptions. The Japanese are an island people who have assimilated certain Chinese, Korean, and American ways, but always in the interest of self-improvement. What seems Westernized in them, what they describe as Western in fact, has been "Japanized," that is, assimilated for their purpose, which is the attainment of perfection in all the passions. The West never had such a goal, not on this earth, at least, and nothing seems more likely to lead us into miscalculations than the proposition that our interests are, in the last analysis, identical with Japan's. We have some interests that are mutual and many, including the ultimate ones, that are not. "We believed the Americans would be perfect," Taeko said once when a group of us were talking about the mistakes of the Occupation.

It seemed that our imperfection, by suggesting the folly of Japanese ambition, had profoundly disillusioned her. And strangely, Taeko had decided I should be made to understand.

About three-thirty A.M. New Year's morning, after passing midnight at a party with my friend, Ray Steinberg, who writes for the *Saturday Evening Post*, I went to Oyuki in the rain. Akasaka was cold and dark except for the warm light under Oyuki's orange awning. The rain drummed on the awning. Janko, dressed in a fragile golden kimono, was sitting by the phone. Four young Japanese in evening clothes and black raincoats hunched over the counter eating good-luck rice cakes. Ami waved the Miles Davis record at me. And Taeko flew into my arms.

She helped me out of my raincoat, giggling nervously about a surprise. Except for the hanging addition of a petrified blowfish and a new lantern, nothing in the little room seemed changed. And for a while, she merely sat with me at the counter, showing me how to eat rice cakes in soup with chopsticks. The taste was like dietetic taffy or stale matzoh balls. Then suddenly, with a flourish, Taeko handed me a small, flat box. My gift: a black necktie for New Year's. She kissed me while Ami and Janko applauded. "Surprise, Tom-san!" she cried.

By five that morning, only we four, the bargirl, the whore, Momma-san, and I remained at Oyuki. Taeko had changed into a red ski jacket, red ski pants, and white boots. Ami pulled on a cloth coat over her thick yellow sweater. And Janko went out and came in again wearing a moth-eaten raincoat. Her room was next door. We found a taxi and drove to the edge of a dimly-lit park not far from the 1964 Olympic grounds. Then, in the rain and predawn chill, with one umbrella for the four of us, we joined some thousands of celebrants on a half-mile walk along a broad gravel path to the Meiji shrine. . . .

I remember it as a fantasy, more awesome than a dream. Our feet crunched on the gravel; thousands of feet crunching on the gravel sounded like the roll of toy snare drums. We marched, huddled in lock-step, within an enormous silent crowd, girls in kimonos, men in street clothes or tuxedos, some without coats, many bareheaded, all trudging head down into the rain. There was a laugh or a giggle now and again, but the crowd was truly silent—and yet you felt everyone was high and happy and excited by the long walk among the strange old trees that lined the pathway. We passed a policeman every fifty yards and one cluster of vendors selling toys, food, and good luck charms. We trooped over a stone bridge, under a carved archway, and into a gray-green light. There were two tents off to one side, one for off-duty policemen, and the other for priests. Then, we entered a bright arena and queued up to face the shrine; it was an exquisite temple with turned-up eaves and a dozen graceful doors open so that we might see the symbolic red boxes inside. A tarpaulin covered the steps leading up to the doors, which were guarded by a temporary wall, about waist-high, keeping everyone outside. When our turn came, we threw a coin over the wall onto the steps, amid thousands of coins, and clapped our hands twice. Then, palms together, we made a prayerful wish for 1965. Taeko pitched her coin beyond the steps onto the shrine floor. The spirits in the boxes probably frowned and forgave her. Janko's toss was more accurate. Both were serious and, not wanting to fail at anything, so was I. Only Ami excused herself. "I am a Roman Catholic," she said.

Later, soaked through by the rain, we came to another arch and moved into a second arena. Sheltered in a booth, a priest wearing a white kimono sold each of us an arrow with white feathers. Hung in our homes, it was guaranteed to protect us from evil spirits. Another priest told our fortune for a few yen: Each of us drew a numbered stick through a small hole in a box full of sticks. Each number was matched by a slip of rice paper in another box. Fortunes were printed on each slip. Taeko's predicted she would find love through patience. Janko's foretold triumph over trouble through will power. Ami's promised happiness via fortitude. Mine saw diligence rewarded by victory. We were all in luck, promised perfection.

At last, we came to an overflowing fountain. We washed our hands and gargled a little to make a clean start in the New Year.

We also reminded ourselves of the tradition that every Japanese must cleanse himself before looking upon the beloved Emperor. Janko, whose face had hard little lines around the eyes and at the corners of her mouth, looked happier than I had ever seen her. And prettier, too, even though her mascara was running. Moreover, for a change, Taeko's cheeks were naturally pink.

In the rain and pale dawn, we returned to a street where vendors were selling good luck tangerines and traditional mementos: The one we bought was an armless and legless little doll with two white spots where his eyes should have been. He, too, guaranteed good luck in the spirit of the mythical Dasi Huda, a Chinese philosopher who had remained seated for ten years in one position trying to think up a new idea. When it came to him, he found that he could no longer use his arms or legs. But his idea was worth it: If you fail at anything, he had said, keep trying eight times and something will be accomplished; if what is accomplished is not what you wanted, keep trying. Happiness will come. An owner of a Dasi Huda doll was to follow this advice, forthwith. Then on the occasion of the first and second happy events of the new year, he was to blacken the doll's respective white eyes so that Dasi Huda might "see."

I gave mine one eye then and there.

Later, at an all-night confectionary, Taeko, Ami, Janko, and I ate chocolate sundaes for breakfast. Then I dropped them at their homes in Akasaka and drove on to my hotel. It was almost eight A.M. Some residents had already come down to the dining room. But the members of the morning hotel staff looked as though they, too, had been out all night. As I hurried across the lobby, one by one, bellboys, clerks, and elevator girls brightened, smiled and enthusiastically wished me a happy new year. In the elevator, I asked the operator why everyone was so glad to see me. She suppressed a giggle and did not answer. But her eyes fell on my white Meiji arrow.

"Happy New Year," she said.

In my room, I gave Dasi Huda his second eye. . . .

Since American prestige was said to require a full complement of strategic and tactical nuclear weapons, I decided to visit among people who had had some experience with the use of such weapons. My schedule allowed only a brief visit to Hiroshima and, as I left, I knew that whatever I might write about it would seem incomplete. In the twentieth year after August 6, 1945, I could tell little about *Pikadon,* the *pika* (lightning) and *don* (thunder) of the atomic bomb, and less about the suffering of *hibakusha,* the survivors of the disaster. Moreover, I could demonstrate no propositions about thermonuclear wars to come. I would not, because the effect of the first atomic bomb—240,000 dead, eighty per cent casualties among 160,000 survivors—could give no real understanding of the probable effect of present-day weapons which might destroy all life on this planet. But, in any case, there would be the people I met and the city I saw.

Sleepless on New Year's morning, two hours by air from Tokyo, I arrived at Hiroshima airport. Leaving the plane, I chanced to meet a resident of Hiroshima and we agreed to share a taxi into town. He was a short, dark man, about forty-five years old, and well-dressed. On his left jaw, there was a pink scar, or rather a blotch, the size of a silver dollar. His English was as American as mine. I have lost his card, but I believe his name was Masamichi Ito. He was in the appliance business. And like myself, he had not enjoyed the bumpy air over western Honshu as we were preparing to land.

In the taxi, Ito and I began talking about our New Year celebrations. He told me his daughter spent a month's salary for her holiday kimono, obi, and sash; and it was only for this season— next year she would certainly buy a new one regardless of the sacrifice. I told him a little about Taeko and he smiled. "It is a good time to be alive," he said. Then it came out that he was one of the *hibakusha.* He said that he had been irradiated two miles from the explosion center and that he had plastic surgery on his jaw for the removal of a keloid scar. Ito had not expected to live twenty years after *Pikadon,* but now he imagined he would collect his three-score and ten.

Ito searched in his pockets until he found a tangerine-colored travel folder illustrated on the cover with a sketch of a girl wearing a spectacular kimono. Admitting that he was a shameless booster of Hiroshima, he urged me to read it. Then he changed his mind and read aloud: "The population of pre-war Hiroshima was four hundred thousand but the bomb reduced it to one-third. With the gradual reconstruction taking shape, the population increased steadily, and it is near five hundred thousand now and the tenth largest city in Japan." Ito paused. "Every word of that is true," he said, "except the reconstruction isn't *gradual* anymore." As he spoke, I was looking out at the city. The weather was good, clear and not too cold. The girls in kimonos were getting by wrapped in short outercoats with fur collars.

At first glance, Hiroshima seemed a provincial Tokyo. It has broad avenues and crooked side streets. The same lovely pennants flap in front of stores and restaurants. The same frantic neon dazzles the eye—MUSHROOM CLOUD SALOON—and depresses the spirit, even in daylight. The same polite, passionate faces are seen in the crowds. What makes a difference are gray-blue mountains everywhere in the background, but even these are defied by telephone lines strung Tokyo-style on black poles instead of underground.

Ito boasted that Hiroshima had to be rebuilt because its site was too valuable to abandon. I would see on a map of Honshu Island that the Ota River has seven mouths forming the delta on which Hiroshima was built at the edge of the Inland Sea. "Geography makes us the major port of western Japan," Ito said. "We've got a Mitsubishi shipyard and a Nippon steel plant, four Rotary clubs and four Lions clubs, skyscrapers and broad avenues, as you can see, and the Hiroshima Carps." The Carps are a Central League professional baseball team that plays both day and night games in a twenty-five thousand seat stadium smack in the middle of baseball-happy Hiroshima. "The Carps always lose," Ito beamed. "But we love them—like the Mets." Ito had seen the New Yorkers play on his last trip to San Francisco.

The taxi had pulled up at the Grand Hotel, but Ito wanted to talk a little longer, so we sat. He spoke rapidly about the death and resurrection of Hiroshima, seemingly for his own benefit as well as mine. He said he was one of the few *hibakusha* who had recovered well enough to make a success in the new Hiroshima. The mayor, Shinzo Hamai, was another. Most, however, had been unable to compete with those post-*Pikadon* citizens who flocked to Hiroshima from all over Japan beginning in the late forties. The outsiders did most of the work of rebuilding the city and reaped the rewards. Many of them now even wanted to change the city's image, emphasizing its industrial promise over its atomic history. But Ito did not agree. He said he was certain that business as usual produces war as usual. "When we stop fearing ourselves," he said, "that's the day the next war begins. It will come the moment we forget the last one. The outsiders don't realize—you can't escape geography." Ito seemed about to drown in an irrepressible wave of sorrow. But he continued, explaining the fact that Hiroshima is closer to the mainland of Asia than any of Japan's major cities, as close to Pusan as London is to Paris. He was certain that it would be a military staging area and munitions center for World War III as it was during Japan's war with Russia, during both world wars, and during the Korean War. "Oh, yes!" Ito exclaimed. "Hiroshima is an eternal target." And that idea seemed almost more than he could bear.

At last, Ito let me go, and just before noon I checked into the Grand Hotel. It is a functional, Hilton-ish place, not far from Hatchobori, the city's business and entertainment district, and close to the Peace Memorial Park as well. The desk clerk assured me that it was the newest hotel in the city and definitely not the older one that Alain Resnais used for *Hiroshima Mon Amour*. Then he sent my bag upstairs, and I went out for a walk.

My first objective was a visit to the exact spot where the Bomb had exploded. But I lost my way and eventually found myself on a hill overlooking the city. The ruins of the original Hiroshima "Carp" Castle (1591-1945) were below me and the rebuilt castle (1958) just behind. Five young men from Kyoto were taking pictures of one another (each with his own camera) against the

Hatchobori skyline. And three generations from the suburbs, grandmother, mother and teen-age daughter, were clinging together as they climbed the hill on nervous feet. I helped them up. The mother said her immediate family had been safely outside of Hiroshima during the war, but anyway, that was a long time ago. Then she kindly pointed out the sights: There was the new justice building, the new police station, the new Toyo-Kogyo motorcycle factory down in the valley, and—oh, yes, the Dome. In the distance, I saw the ruin of Hiroshima's prewar industrial exhibition hall with the black girders of its dome exposed to the sky. It is very close to the explosion center, the mother said, and was left standing as a memorial after all other bombed-out structures were demolished to make way for the rebuilding of the city. This was to be my moment of greatest intensity in Hiroshima. From the remains of the castle that was the beginning of this town, it is a long, long mile to the Atomic Dome. The space between is tightly packed. There are new houses, shops, office buildings, the Grand Hotel, and many cars—front bumpers decorated with tangerines and pine boughs for the New Year. Consider all of it devastation and emptiness again! Thinking about the bomb exploding, I had always imagined myself at ground zero; but it may be possible only on the *circumference*— barely possible—to think about one death at a time up to two hundred thousand or to think of megatons landing on New York.

At one o'clock, I returned to the hotel to keep a luncheon appointment I had made by phone from Tokyo with one of the mayor's aides, Kaoru Ogura, head of the Foreign Affairs Section at City Hall. He was a tall man, blithe and trim, in his early forties. He was not one of the *hibakusha,* but he had lived many years in Hiroshima and knew the people.

Ogura and I ate in Hatchobori in a small restaurant which had an inlaid hot-plate at each table. A complete meal with saki and tea costs about fifty cents, but you had to cook your own beef and vegetables. While preparing our food, Ogura said he believed Hiroshima was a good place to live. He liked the air and also the people, even though there had been severe problems of discrimination against the *hibakusha* minority. A few years back, the majority tended to look upon them as freaks, at best, and dangerous to the public health, at worst. Survivors had trouble getting jobs and still more trouble finding mates—no marriage bureau would accept their applications. They were even barred from the public baths. But, more and more, Ogura said, the memory of the Bomb was fading. A long battle has been fought to provide medical care and other benefits for the *hibakusha*, and most of them had achieved a reasonably satisfactory physical condition. "We have a special hospital for the victims," Ogura said, "with one hundred beds always full—mostly cases of blood disease. Forty or fifty die every year, really more than we expected after twenty years. But still, the survivors are surviving. They marry and raise families—they have to live and rebuild."

Ogura became cautious when I asked about politics. He said the strongest political feeling in Hiroshima is antiwar rather than anti-American. "In general," he said, "eight out of ten survivors do not accuse the United States. They can be led to say you shouldn't have dropped the bomb, but this is still Japan. Hiroshima was a disaster, true; but we are accustomed to many disasters. We are resigned. That is Buddhism—a philosophy of resignation. All of the peace agitation comes from perhaps one out of five people. They are people either particularly religious and therefore strongly antiwar or else they are communists and automatically anti-American. But let me tell you. Few of the *hibakusha* are like this. They do nothing. They belong to nothing. They don't give a damn about the peace movement. Hiroshima is supposed to be a Mecca of peace, but it isn't. If you want a peace meeting here, you'd better schedule it for August 6. We tried to have a disarmament rally not long ago, hired a big hall, and got a hundred old ladies to come. The truth is that the use of Hiroshima as a symbol of peace hardly affects us at all. We are all opposed to the Bomb. But then who isn't?"

In Ogura's car after lunch, we drove around Hatchobori. Most of the major Japanese banks own branches in the district. Two new skyscrapers were in the process of construction. And the number of bars—the Bourbon, the Florida, the Jazz Club, the Apollo, for example—seemed sufficient for a metropolis twice the size of Hiroshima. Defensively, Ogura said: "We are a commercial city." Next, we visited Peace Memorial Park, a scattering of memorials on a vast plain. In the center, on a graveled walk, there is a steel cenotaph. The Atomic Dome arises at one end, just beyond a finger of the Ota River. And at the opposite end, there are three large concrete and glass buildings—a research center and the New Hiroshima Hotel (the one that *was* part of the scene in *Hiroshima Mon Amour*) flanking the Peace Memorial Museum. The Park was originally conceived by Kenzo Tange, who later designed the buildings for the Tokyo Olympic games. According to his concept, one should be able to stand at the museum, look down the long walk, see through the opening in the cenotaph (which, very roughly, resembles the upper half of a covered wagon) and, without obstruction, view the Dome silhouetted against the sky. But recently, despite Tange's opposition, an eternal flame had been placed between the cenotaph and the Dome. Moreover, the Chamber of Commerce and Industry built a glassy skyscraper on a piece of land *behind* the Dome, wrecking the vista. Some members of the Chamber even suggested the Dome itself was an eyesore and ought to be torn down but, so far, they had been thwarted.

There was a sign on the museum door announcing its holiday schedule: it would be closed until January 3. So Ogura and I strolled around the mall watching scores of students, nuns, young lovers, country folk, and city families come and go. Some were subdued but none were austere. Some bowed and prayed at the cenotaph or rang the memorial gong. But most seemed rather more inquisitive than involved. Tirelessly, the Japanese photographed one another under a bright-hazy, F-16, hundredth-of-a-second afternoon sun. "The Park is becoming a place for people to take their leisure," Ogura said. "I think that's good. It should not be too serious."

At dusk, Ogura dropped me at the hotel. He said he would arrange for me to see the mayor and the director of the Chamber

of Commerce and Industry in a day or two. Then he wished me a
Happy New Year and drove off. I killed some time in the hotel
lobby watching a rock-and-roll telecast from Tokyo; with sub-
titles, the program could have gone on a U.S. network any afternoon at five. After dark, I walked downtown to find a Chinese
dinner. Although most of the restaurants were closed for the holiday, the movies were lit up like nothing between Honshu and
Hollywood. There was "Circus World" with a giant pop-art
poster of John Wayne, and Burt Lancaster in "The Train." One
double feature combined a Doris Day with a Natalie Wood. And
the only Japanese film, wildly advertised with pennants, stream-
ers, and gory pictures, was a samurai Western. I walked along the
arcades and side streets that feed into the main avenues of the
district. Every hundred yards or so, there was a pinball palace
where crowds of expressionless young men in tight suits and girls
in holiday kimonos methodically flipped steel balls into vertical
machines hoping to win a can of shaving soap, a chocolate bar, or
a pack of cigarettes. The name of the game was *pachinko*, designed for the thrill of fast play and an incredible number of near-
misses. In Hiroshima, as in Tokyo, pachinko was a rage, a mania,
and an antidote, perhaps, for the Nippon-style rat race. I bought
a bucket of balls, played for half an hour, and won a box of
cookies. Later, I ate the cookies for dessert in a Chinese restaurant while watching a dubbed telecast of "Bonanza." I was de-
lighted to hear Ben, Hoss, Little Joe, and Sheriff Coffee speaking
Japanese.

Bright and early next morning, I finally found the spot, *the*
spot, above which the Bomb had gone off. It is a few hundred
yards behind the Atomic Dome, not far from the new Chamber
of Commerce building. Morbidly, I looked up, saw only the sky,
and felt ridiculous.

Then I walked along the upper border of the Peace Park beside
the river into a shabby zone of jerry-built shacks largely inhabited
by *hibakusha*. A tattered man standing knee-deep in a pile of
rags, cardboard boxes, old bottles, and other invaluable rubbish

leaned on the handle of his pushcart and waved to me. His name was Masao Tamura. He said after twenty years he didn't think much about the Bomb. "I lost many relatives," he said, "but I myself was occupying Indonesia at the time."

Further on there was a man chopping wood in the dooryard of a well-kept shack. A poster tacked up near the door showed a dove of peace attacking a Polaris submarine and workers kicking capitalists in a struggle for cash. The woodchopper, dressed in a T-shirt and coveralls, carried his logs inside and returned to invite me for tea. We sat in a small, neat office with a kettle on the stove and more posters on the walls. One was a National Liberal Laborers Union election announcement showing my host, Haruo Ogami. It bore the legend: "Good life for all union people." Apparently, he had been elected president of his local. Ogami was a gentle, strong-looking man, age thirty-eight. The morning of *Pikadon*, he was a city fireman on call about three miles from the explosion center. "I was in a concrete, sheltered place," he told me, "protected above but not below the waist. When I woke up, the lower half of my body was paralyzed. I hate the American government that did that. I spent five years in the hospital but now I move around pretty well. I get stiff and itchy in hot weather ... Yes, I like living in Hiroshima. It's quite changed since before the war. Many more tourists come but also a new gangster element ... No, I'm not married. I can't find a woman to take care of me. And, anyway, I don't want to take a chance on having a child." He said he had read an authoritative report based on a study of six thousand births in Hiroshima and Nagasaki, 1948-1954, indicating genetic damage due to irradiation was "of little clinical consequence." Then he smiled. "But I know," he said, "I may not be strong enough to support family life. And something could be wrong with my children. So I devote my life to the union. I only want to communicate peace to the world."

Ogami later presented me with a gift—his own ball-point pen. It was red and white plastic and soon ran out of ink.

About half past ten, a taxi delivered me to a joyless little building near the edge of Hatchobori. Professor Ichiro Moritaki met me at the door and ushered me into his headquarters. He taught ethics at Hiroshima University, but spent most of his time trying to activate a new peace organization called Gensuikin. He was an original founder of Gensuikyo, Japan's first nationwide council of *hibakusha,* religious sects, unions, political parties, and women's committees opposed to the Bomb. In the fifties, before political differences tore it apart, Gensuikyo helped collect more than thirty million signatures on petitions condemning atomic testing. By 1963, however, elements sympathetic to Red China had gained control—and, like many Buddhists, Protestants, Democratic Socialists, pro-Soviet communists, and others, Professor Moritaki quit. But he continued to operate out of Gensuikyo's local headquarters because no one would put him out. His office was a small, seedy room with a coal stove, blackboard, and four desks piled high with pamphlets and posters. An intense, formal man, Moritaki had a white mane and gray mustache. He was very tall and thin. *Pikadon* had cost him an eye and its replacement gave him a distracted look. Seated at the stove, we talked for an hour or so about the difference between Gensuikyo and Gensuikin. Finally, he arrived at the essence of it. *He* opposed all nuclear testing. *They* opposed all testing except in "socialist" countries, especially China. "I was very happy about the test-ban treaty," Moritaki said. "When I first got the news, I rushed to the Atomic Bomb Hospital to tell the people about it. But the communists in Gensuikyo said the treaty was a fraud and a camouflage to keep China from getting the Bomb." He sprang to the blackboard and punctuated his words with Japanese characters that I couldn't read. He was fed up with politics, he said. Now he wanted to rebuild the peace movement with individual volunteers, especially *hibakusha,* and not parties or groups or foreign interests. He knew what had to be done:

"Two years ago," Professor Moritaki said, "I made a sit-down strike before the cenotaph in Peace Park protesting the resumption of nuclear testing by the United States. I sat there twelve days and twelve nights. I am a Buddhist of the Zen sect, so I am used to this. Thirty thousand people came to see me and I told them I was friendly to the United States but loathed her nuclear policy. I loathe all power politics. And while I was sitting there, a little girl came to me with a question.

" 'Can you stop a nuclear test merely by sitting down here?' she asked.

"It was a great question to me. This meant—'Can your peace movement stop preparation for a nuclear war?' I thought and I meditated about this great question. I envisioned a chain reaction of human minds, a world wide effort to stop these nuclear policies. A chain reaction of spiritual atoms would defeat the chain reaction of material atoms! This was my answer to the little girl and to all the people of Japan."

Professor Moritaki wanted to be sure I wrote that down.

"A-chain-reaction-of-spiritual-atoms," he said, "must-defeat-the chain-reaction-of-material-atoms."

That afternoon, I rented a two-door Datsun and drove myself around Hijiyama Park to Ujina, the port of Hiroshima. I stopped at the last boat dock for an unobstructed view of the sea and the mountains. The sun was very bright and warm. The water sparkled and the mountains looked like charcoal. A schoolboy in uniform joined me, watching the ships steam south toward Shikoku and Kyushu. He spoke very little English, but I gathered he was attending secondary school and hoped one day to be a nautical engineer.

Again that night, Hatchobori's amusements were limited, but the tempo had picked up. I chose a place called the Grill for dinner and found myself in the midst of a New Year's party for the younger employees of a local insurance company. About twenty couples sat cross-legged in their stocking feet around two long, low tables. They were clapping and shouting as one young man performed a samurai dance using a waiter's tray for a sword. When I joined in the clapping, he leaped over the table to continue his dance in front of me. He executed several stumbling turns and flat-footed leaps. Then, for his finale, he dropped the tray, spun on his heel and fell back into my arms. There was an uncertain wave of applause. Apologetically, he ordered beer and offered me a glass. The room fell silent.

"Cheers!" he said, shyly.

"Happy New Year," I replied.

The young man turned excitedly to his companions. Relieved, they shouted: *"Banzai! Banzai!"*

I raised my glass. They shouted, still louder:

"Banzai! Banzai!"

"Happy New Year!" I said.

"Happy New Year!" they cried. *"Banzai!"*

The following morning at ten, Mayor Shinzo Hamai and Kaoru Ogura visited me at my hotel. The Mayor was a tall, distinguished-looking *hibakusha* in his sixties, who had guided the reconstruction of Hiroshima for most of the past twenty years. We sat in the lobby with a tea service between us and talked for a time about the Gensuikyo-Gensuikin split. Mayor Hamai said it was permanent and that he himself sympathized with Professor Moritaki. In any case, he said, he was more concerned these days with the future of Hiroshima. He wanted the city to become the core of a great urban, suburban, and rural metropolis. "The problems of this city are those of any urban complex," he said. "In the center, which was devastated, we are modern. But we are surrounded by the old-fashioned. We must modernize. Everything must be modernized. If so, we will become *the* center of western Japan." Thus, fervently, he spoke until precisely ten-thirty. Then, Ogura escorted him to City Hall and returned with Yoshiharu Oban, director of the Chamber of Commerce and Industry. Oban was a big man, about fifty, with gold teeth in front and cuff links to match. He was born in Hiroshima, moved away before the *Pikadon,* and returned three months after. Talking to me, he quickly picked up where the Mayor had left off. "It was believed that there would be no trees and no people in Hiroshima for seventy-five years," he said. "But we restored everything in ten years. We are very proud of this. The need now is for more organized culture, more civilization, art museums, theaters, a concert hall. Hiroshima is not the Wild West anymore. We have come through twenty years of adolescence. Now we go into our adult phase. This is our goal: to become the fourth largest city in

Japan." When I asked Oban his opinion of the Atomic Dome, he did not answer specifically. Rather, he said he thought it was a good tourist attraction. "We will keep it, maybe," he said, flashing a golden smile.

After Oban and Ogura had gone, I loaded my bags into the Datsun, checked out of the hotel, and drove into Hatchobori for lunch. The streets were jammed with holiday shoppers. In front of Tenmaya Department Store, three old ladies and two old men were playing cheerfully tuneless music on assorted makeshift instruments. They wore brilliant red shirts, striped baseball knickers, and yellow caps—with open umbrellas strapped to their backs advertising the Diamuru Department Store, Tenmaya's competition down the street. The crowds moved around them, surging into Tenmaya, laying seige to counters piled high with merchandise, moving up and up, floor by glutted floor, to the roof which opened onto an elaborate playground. While men did most of the shopping on the floors below, children under the eyes of their mothers rode the ferris wheel, rocketships, and satellites. There were long lines waiting for each attraction and a crowd six deep around a snack bar that served, among other things, excellent hamburgers.

About three o'clock that afternoon, I parked the car beside a gay fountain near the museum in the Peace Park. It seemed that Kenzo Tange had designed the museum to provide shelter for people on the ground level and to emphasize the uniqueness of the floor above. The building is a long, single-story rectangle cantilevered on square pylons. I walked under, and then up a long, open flight of stairs to the museum level. A guard presented me with a transistor device for listening to an English description as I passed from one exhibit to the next. Then, along with about twenty-five other visitors, I was on my own. Here were the familiar black-and-white photographs of the *Pikadon* sky over Hiroshima filled with debris, the first-aid station crammed with the wounded, the child with his legs ulcerated and peeling, the horrid close-ups of enormous keloid scars, and the panorama of disaster looking across the ruins toward the mountains. There were also glass cases filled with irradiated clothing, bottles melted into grotesque shapes, gnarled chunks of steel, slivers of wood embedded in concrete, shattered bones, and a pitifully twisted bicycle. At the end, I returned my transistor and walked out.

The museum had tried to show human suffering on a new threshold, something previously unimaginable, and thus turn us against our weapons. But in this, for me, it failed. You felt pity and fear at the sight of so much tragedy. But there were really no new notions or clues or insights at the museum. I could only find them, if at all, in the new Hiroshima.

At dusk, I returned to my car and drove a long way around to the airport. I again passed the Mushroom Cloud Saloon. It had not yet opened for the night.

Back in Tokyo, I spent the rest of the week working off a full schedule of interviews with Japanese businessmen, labor leaders, politicians, and intellectuals. Their themes were monotonously similar. Each disavowed anti-Americanism and then, according to his own light, took exception to most of America's military, political, and economic policies in Asia. In general they were against war and in favor of profitable coexistence with everyone, including China.

The wisest among them seemed to be Kenzo Tange, the peerless architect, who told me one day that he sensed a growing concern here for "the home environment," a desire to be relieved of foreign tensions in order to concentrate on Japan's on-rushing urban crisis. "Most foreign problems are domestic anyway," Tange said. He was a shy, tiny man with a flair for dialectical epigrams. In the next thirty-five years, Tange said, Japan's urban population would increase two-and-a-half times. Total population would rise only from 93,000,000 to 120,000,000. But added to this normal growth the movement from rural areas to the cities would completely change the condition of life. One hundred million people would live in cities in the year 2000 as opposed to 53,000,000 now. The Tokyo-Osaka-Nagoya complex alone would increase its population from 28,000,000 to about 80,000,000. Tange estimated the maintainance of economic growth over this period would require an investment forty times greater than the investment of the past twenty years. He anticipated no great *financial* obstacles, but he foresaw an enormous threat of confusion and chaos. "The worst thing," he said, "is the brain of the political people. The question is not money, but how to spend money. As of this moment, even Tokyo does not have a city planning committee."

A few days before I was to leave for Djakarta, the Indonesians withdrew from the United Nations. And I received a wire from my wife: "WASHINGTON OFFICE INDONESIAN AMBASSADOR REGRETS SUKARNO UNABLE TO SEE YOU DUE TO PRESENT STATE OF AFFAIRS. STOP. SORRY. STOP. YOU MAY WANT TO TRY FOR MAO TSE-TUNG."

I decided to ignore my clever wife.

That same day, Shigeto Tsuru invited me to come to his home for afternoon tea. Feeling very special, I arrived about four, entering through a gate in a wall that concealed Tsuru's beloved garden from passersby. The house was one of four in a compound on half-an-acre of real estate valued at fifty million yen, or about $140,000. Tsuru earned eighty-five thousand yen (less than $250) a month at the university, while the cost of living in Tokyo was perhaps half again as expensive as New York. But, as he explained, his wife had won five hundred thousand yen in a lottery in 1950 with which they had bought their piece of land. Then they divided it into four plots and sold three of them, respectively, to Mrs. Tsuru's mother, aunt, and brother-in-law, using this money to build their own small eight-room bungalow. Since then, the value of the land had gone up more than one hundred times. Inside, there was one room maintained in the traditional floor-level Japanese style. The rest were "Western." Books flowed over from the study into the bedroom. And a shame-faced television set occupied an obscure corner in the living room. Tsuru assured me he had *borrowed* the TV. He said he spent his leisure time gardening, playing croquet in the compound with his nephews, or reading his periodicals. Within five days of publication, he would receive the New York *Times Sunday Review,* *Daedalus, The New Stateman,* and *The Correspondent.* The TV was for his wife's amusement, to look at when, as often happened, her husband appeared on interview programs. "The day that President Kennedy was shot," Tsuru recalled, "our journalists were up at four in the morning to witness the first pre-Olympics experiment with Telstar. The assassination was Telstar's first broadcast to us. I was called for my comments and wound up that day on eight television and radio shows."

Mrs. Tsuru was a small, bright, intense woman. She served tea and sweetcakes. Then Tsuru and I settled down in comfortable chairs in the living room for our final chat. He wanted to talk first about the psychological effect of our aid programs. The Sixties had been an interesting decade thus far, he said, because the time had come to rethink some of our most cherished beliefs, such as the concept of economic assistance. It was time to let nations see what they could do for themselves: "After all," Tsuru said, "Japan 'took-off' between 1858 and 1900 borrowing only three million dollars to finance the Tokyo-Yokohama railroad. Except for this, we developed ourselves, perhaps because we were not bound by strict or orthodox religiosity like most Catholic or Buddhist countries . . . United States' aid leads nations to expect miracles. Your publicity makes it seem to the recipients that something big has happened."

Politicians, when in doubt, spend money, I said.

"Well, it is a fact that aid *saps* self-help energy. One of India's leading economists has said the same thing. He told the Americans: 'Stop giving us aid!' Sukarno has said it. Nasser has said it."

"The aid program worked so well in Europe, it seemed a good idea to extend it to underdeveloped countries."

"It is not a bad idea," Tsuru said. "But it must be re-thought."

I told Tsuru I had heard a great deal of criticism of U.S. policy in Japan. Yet differences of opinion on policy hardly accounted for the emotional anti-Americanism among Japanese intellectuals.

Attempting to explain, Tsuru generalized from his own experience in the Thirties. He said that prewar Japan had had so little information about America that it was natural for intellectuals to have a low opinion of American science and to feel that American literature was inferior to the works of Stendhal, Mann, Galsworthy, Tolstoy, Ibsen, Molnar, and Dostoevski. There was a well-developed prejudice that assumed Americans were rich and charitable but culturally inferior to Europeans.

"Some exceptions were made," Tsuru said, "but this prejudice was the reason that so few of us went to America to study. And these few, like myself, almost always went by accident. Shunsuke Tsurumi, who is now professor of philosophy at Kyoto University, went to the United States by accident and discovered Pierce, James, and Dewey. But his was a rare experience. Now, today, of course, very many of us go expressly to the United States for study."

Tsuru offered me a *Hope* cigarette and took one for himself. He was a determined smoker. He thought for a while. Then he got up, went into his study, and returned with two passports. He placed them on the table between us.

"Given the fact that large numbers of Japanese are left-wing," he began, "one emotional element here is that so many of us have been denied visas to the United States. You Americans spread a very big net to catch a very few fish. Many honest, democratic, liberal progressives have been denied visas. And when some of them do get visas, after waiting six months, they get only special 'single-entry' visas so that they cannot even go over to the Canadian side of Niagara Falls. It has all been so arbitrary. Two men here of the same standing apply and one gets a visa in a week, while the other waits six months. Then they ask themselves, why is America so suspicious? This spreads an emotional reaction among intellectuals. And the two men decide America is bigoted and not worth visiting anyway.

"Lately, the University of Okinawa invited a scholar in ancient

Japanese literature to lecture. He had criticized American policy, and so the American authorities of Okinawa denied him a visa. There was a tremendous protest from Okinawan students and, finally, two months later, he got the visa.

"But, when this happens a hundred times a year, to one or two professors in every college, a general antagonism develops toward the United States. In fact, the feeling grows that anyone who *does* accept an invitation to an American university is a collaborator with the U.S. Government. On an intellectual level, we may simply agree or disagree with your visa procedure. But there is also the emotional reaction."

Tsuru held up the passports he had retrieved from his study. One was his; the other belonged to his wife. On the occasion of his two postwar visits to the United States, he had had to wait more than three months for each visa. And both times, he received a single-entry visa, while his wife received a multi-entry visa.

"Apparently, there is a code number that tells the authorities that I am a man to be watched," he said. "In my own case, I do not resent it. But many Japanese do, and refuse to go to the States . . . It has a very wide effect. In 1962, there was a conference of Japanese and American businessmen and intellectuals at Dartmouth University. One man who was invited is president of a major rayon company here, a highly respected businessman whose crime was that he had sold a chemical fibers plant to mainland China. The Japanese government had not been happy about this sale because it involved a five-year deferred payment, which was tantamount to economic aid for China, in our government's view. But the sale was made. And when it came time for the businessman to request a visa for America, the U.S. consul in his hometown started to investigate his political associations. When this became known, the businessman protested to Ambassador Reischauer, who was outraged and put a stop to the investigation. Yet, at Dartmouth, the businessman had to say that it was this sort of thing that damaged Japanese-American relations. And it does. I have been through it and have nothing to hide. But neither does many a Japanese intellectual whose rational convictions are aggravated and magnified by such treatment."

Tsuru spoke so calmly, with such gravity, that I found myself responding similarly. It was as if we two were speaking of a third person who was not well. We hoped for his recovery, but we did have to face up to the fact that he was sick.

"Now all this is related to the fact that it is not easy to accept another man's benevolence graciously," Tsuru continued, "especially when the benefactor's background, his whole aspect, is not understood. There is an expression here—*to slap one's cheek with a bundle of bank notes.* The United States does not intend to slap anyone's cheek, I know, but many Japanese feel that it does. They are not sure your benefactions are genuine, that the giving of money by the various foundations does not have an ulterior motive. I believe the Japanese are wrong about this, but they do not understand the tradition of Ford and Rockefeller and the rest. So, when a foundation gives a study-grant of one hundred thousand dollars, the Japanese become suspicious. A Japanese-sponsored grant is usually on the order of a hundred dollars or a thousand dollars. You give an enormous sum and we ask: What are the Americans up to? Can I accept their grant without becoming indebted? Am I being baited to give some political cooperation? These questions extend into the sphere of exchange programs sponsored by your State Department. All these programs are suspect. Are you trying to put something over on us? Won't acceptance brand us as a collaborator?

"You see, there is a reservoir of Japanese-American good will and part of it has been due to grants for Japanese intellectuals. Those who support Japan's present foreign policy, which for all practical purposes is identical with American foreign policy, find no trouble accepting your generosity. But those who criticize Japan's foreign policy feel that such people have been bought by American money. I myself believe in the integrity of the Ford, Rockefeller, and Asian foundations. But because of the emotional situation, it is felt here that these foundations have varying political implications. A Rockefeller grantee is felt to be neutral. A

Ford grantee is felt to be somewhat political. And the Asian Foundation grantee is felt to be most political. If an American comes here under a grant from the Asian Foundation, he may even be boycotted by many intellectual groups."

Was Tsuru expressing his own opinion about the foundations or reporting the opinions of others?

With a wave of his hand, displaying a trace of professional impatience, he answered: "I, Tsuru, feel no difference between Rockefeller and Ford. But I feel the Asian Foundation has probably had the express purpose of *winning friends* for America. And this has political implications. We Japanese are often naive. But when Americans do not see the political implications of winning friends, *you* are being naive and many Japanese are suspicious of such naivete."

Tsuru was not quite finished, but he had decided it was time for us to stroll in his winter garden. We walked among fine shrubs and perfect grass to the gate, and back again. He spoke once more of the Japanese "dichotomy," the contrast between private beauty and public ugliness in modern Japan. But now he related it to anti-American feelings. Japanese intellectuals often identified public ugliness with cultural influences from the United States. "There are manifestations of American civilization that Japanese intellectuals deeply resent," he said. "In a few words, these can be summed up by Hollywood and the television series. Once you have visited America, you know that there is a far greater intensity of intellectuality in Greenwich Village than there is anywhere in Japan. But out of ignorance and irrationality, the Japanese intellectual thinks America is *anti*-intellectual. He resents the Coca-Colonization of Japan. He will not go to an American film even if he hears it is a good one. He will not own a TV set. He will denounce rock-and-roll jazz. It all blends together in a general difference of attitude toward life—many people here feel that the open, friendly, frank American way of life is strange, just as Americans often feel the suppressed, sometimes silly behavior of the Japanese is strange. But we put together American openness with the sinister American effort at thought control—as evidenced by the visa situation—and this contradiction itself forms a basis for suspicion and hostility. The United States is the standard that we all look to in order to measure our own economic and political development, and yet here is this contradiction. That is my point. . . ."

I had given up on Akira Kuroyanagi, chief of the General Overseas Bureau of Sokagakkai. But at ten in the morning on my next to last day in Japan, he called to say his president, Daisaku Ikeda, would see me. I was to bring a list of questions by noon to the Sokagakkai headquarters in Shinjuku. Akira said I must remember that the interview was "exceptional" and could not last more than thirty minutes.

I found Akira waiting for me outside a small but stately new building. We took off our shoes, slipped into leather sandals, and walked up a flight to the president's paneled, air-conditioned conference room. Moments later, Ikeda joined us. He was a short, stocky, good-looking man with a kind of aggressive sincerity reminiscent of the young Jimmy Hoffa. We sat down around a glass-topped table and were promptly served orange soda and American-made cigarettes.

During the preliminaries, Ikeda told me he had joined Sokagakkai in 1947 at age nineteen when the group's total membership numbered less than thirty. He said he had been prompted "by fear of the struggle between communism" and what he called "spiritualism," which was his essential word for Sokagakkaism. You could not imagine Ikeda suffering a moment's fear in his life, but he took pains to establish fear as his motive: "With the war over," he said, "Japan had to become a peaceful nation. I saw that religion was the only way to prevent another war."

He spoke slowly, with an air of military formality. The death of President Kennedy had made him sad. "I was very sorry," he said. "President Kennedy was a most skillful politician and the most powerful man in the world. I am a youth and the leader of three million youths in our movement. He was a youth, too. Both President Kennedy and I had a desire to make a peaceful world. If I could have met with him, the problems of Asia would have been solved, because I could have told him everything having to do with peace. I want to stress that all politicians have a bad idea in their stomachs. They believe in power politics. But I was very respectful of President Kennedy's use of power and appreciated his spiritualism, his Catholicism. He wanted to make a peaceful world."

The spiritual and moral tone of the United States, however, had left Ikeda with mixed feelings. "America gives more respect to the individual than Japan," he said. "But I regret you have a bad idea about the black man. In America, democracy is flourishing. But you must develop the democratic ideology to respect Negroes. If you do this, your nation will flourish more and more. I visited the United States several times and studied the Catholic Church. I know all about the purity of the Catholic Church. But the Church takes money from the poor. This is the delinquency of the Church and a problem that must be solved. We believe it is wrong to raise funds from poor people. Money should come from the rich man. This is the natural thing. And I mean this not only for your Catholic Church, but for all churches. Otherwise, there will always be a great gap in the church between the rich man and the poor man."

Ikeda folded his arms and closed his eyes. When he opened them again, he had changed the subject. "The Japanese way is to have each person think about his own house," Ikeda said, "but this does not improve democracy. In the Soviet Union, national power is used to suppress the people and you cannot respect this. But the United States, having established its own democracy, does not have a large enough vision of the world. You never lost a war, so you have a foreign policy of militarism . . . But there will be spiritual reconstruction in Japan if we promote good nationalism, as in Sokagakkai. The Soviet Union must send her people throughout the world because without connection with other nations, she will perish. And the United States needs a larger mind to think more deeply about other nations."

"What about China?" I asked.

"Red China must also cooperate with other nations," he said. "She must respect other nations. If she is solitary, she will perish too."

The future of Japanese-American relations troubled Ikeda for several reasons, the most important of which was our failure to understand Sokagakkai. "I agree that the American occupation of Japan was necessary," he said, "if it was necessary to occupy Japan to insure the peace of the world. But now there is no airplane, no battleship, no army from America needed here. You no longer need bases in Japan because you have the atomic submarine. I know all about the atomic submarine. It can be based in your own country and it will still achieve your end. You must understand how the people feel. American policy toward Japan is almost good, but it concentrates too much on capitalists and politicians and not enough on the people. Sokagakkai has big numbers and unless you know *us*, you cannot attain your goal of cooperation with Japan. I am the leader of everyday Japanese people. New things are happening here. And if the leader of your nation disregards Sokagakkai, he will misunderstand our political party and our nation. If you cannot catch the soul of the people, you are defeated.

"Our people are against militarism. Our idea of nationalism is not based on military strength, but on the happiness of the individual Japanese person. This makes Sokagakkai nationalism different from Shinto-Japanese nationalism, which brought war. Our nationalism starts from Buddhism, with mercy to make everything happy for human beings. We want to cooperate with all countries, with the United Nations, in a policy of global racialism."

For Ikeda, it seemed, "global racialism" meant the brotherhood of man. He said critics of Sokagakkai, writing for American newspapers and magazines, had committed a major offense against this concept. They professed to see precisely the "militaristic nationalism" in Sokagakkai that he said he opposed.

" 'A beautiful woman will have resentment from others,' " Ikeda said, " 'and a successful man will have resentment from a failure.' That is an old Japanese proverb. We have about one hundred eighty thousand religious sects in Japan. Among these are wrong ones and right ones. Now, from a scientific point of view and from a Buddhist point of view, it must be realized that Sokagakkai is the right-est one. We want a revolution in religion so we are, of course, going to be criticized. But we have a democratic philosophy. We have had lots of criticism in Japan and, very regrettably, in the United States, which is a big country and judges everything scientifically. Someday, I hope the attitude of the American press will be changed. After all, when Christ, Marx, or Lenin wanted success, they were criticized. From the true Buddha, we believe strongly that every people will respect Sokagakkai because our members recover from their sufferings. About twenty years ago, we had only thirty members. Today, we have millions. This fact proves that our religion is right. If we were not right, we would perish from criticism. But we grow, year by year. Japan as an Asian country is deeply connected with Buddhism. We know the flower of the lotus will bloom after one thousand years. And so, our religion, conceived hundreds of years ago, is now flourishing in Japan. This is the law of nature. Christianity and communism have a strange viewpoint toward us. The time will come when you regret your lack of understanding. . . ."

Early that evening, I dropped into Oyuki to say goodbye to Taeko. When she heard I was leaving next day, she giggled and her eyes filled with tears.

Later, at a restaurant in Akasaka, I ate tempura for dinner with two Tokyo University graduate students. One was Otaka, a bright lad working for a law degree who had recently spent a year at the University of Wisconsin. The other was Noriko, a taut, slender girl with a magpie hairdo and a jacket-sweater-slacks-boots ensemble all in black. Noriko was a sculptress. She had studied at the Brooklyn Museum School of Art and once lived in Greenwich Village not far from my own address on Charles Street. Both Noriko and Otaka participated in the Tokyo riots in 1960 against the U.S.-Japan security pact. When Sukarno visited Tokyo, Noriko shoved a bouquet of flowers in his hand. But she, like Otaka, had been a teen-ager at the time; now they were both twenty-four years old. Otaka had since moved from radical Marxism to Democratic Socialism. In his opinion, Shigeto Tsuru was one of the world's great economists. "I never met him," Otaka said, "but I read his works and often see him on television." Noriko had no heroes anymore. After 1960, her interest in politics flickered out. In New York, she decided that all politics were ugly. New York was ugly, too, and once, on Charles Street, she had attempted suicide.

The three of us spent a curious evening together. At first, they were determined to show me what was most bizarre in Tokyo, so we spent several hours drinking Asahi beer in two tiny saloons, one operated by lesbians, the other by male homosexuals. But then we moved on to a non-alcoholic cellar bar called the Village Gate where we sat at a small table among jazz buffs, drinking Cokes and listening to records by Art Blakey, Louis Armstrong, Coleman Hawkins, and Miles Davis. Otaka did most of the talking. He was sorely disillusioned, having lost faith in Marxism without finding a satisfying substitute. He clung to a faint hope for the future of "socialism" in China, but he did not like the Chinese either. Sipping his Coke, he told me he did not like what was happening anywhere in the world, but especially in the United States.

"You preach," he said, "but you are not solving your own problems. At Wisconsin, I never saw so many happy-minded people. They are happy, because they are so far from any place where you must worry about the Bomb."

"Did you meet anyone you liked?"

"I met Americans I liked. But your government—you are responsible for the isolation of China."

"You're contradictory, Otaka-san. You set up America as an impossible standard of purity and complain because we are not pure."

"Well, you are not pure."

About three A.M., without explaining, Otaka said goodnight and left us at the Village Gate. Noriko laughed.

"This evening was like being in a madhouse listening to two inmates," she said.

"Why?"

"Don't ask me—my head is empty. We are at zero. The old world is through, but nobody can think up a new one. That's why I jumped out of the window on Charles Street."

"You muffed it."

"I landed on my feet, broke a toe, and went back to work. I worked with wood rather than clay. I carve because I want to find the soul in a piece of wood."

At five A.M., Noriko and I ate breakfast in an all-night cafe. Then about six, we picked up my luggage and went to the airport. As I boarded the plane for Hong Kong, I could see her high up on the observation deck, bundled against the cold, waving.

4
Indonesians

Five weeks out of New York, flying from Bangkok to Djakarta, I read an issue of *Time* magazine cover to cover. First after the "Letters" came "The Nation" and "The World," then "The Hemisphere," "People," "The Law," "Medicine," and so on to "Books." Under each heading, the news fell into neat compartments like so many ice cubes in a tray. Lyndon B. Johnson had outlined his program for the Great Society in his first State of the Union message as an elected President. Congressmen murmured about America's involvement in Vietnam. Secretary of State Dean Rusk told them "there are no present plans for escalating the war into North Vietnam. . . ." Various state governors complained about state problems, mostly fiscal. "Off last week on Japan Air Lines' Flight 800 flew Premier Eisaku Sato" to explain to Washington Japan's growing trade with Red China. Charles de Gaulle ordered his Finance Minister to convert seven hundred million U.S. dollars into gold thereby inflating world gold prices and sending shivers through the world money market. And President Sukarno announced Indonesia's withdrawal from the United Nations, heating up speculation about a Djakarta-Peking "coup de grace (for) the West's remaining position in all Asia."

On the night of January 11, when the Indonesian rainy season was a week old, I landed at Kemajoran Airport in Djakarta. A wall of water separated the plane from the terminal building seventy-five yards away. Taking a deep breath, I set off for shore. Then I stopped halfway under a strange compulsion to recheck my visa. The rain washed over the page, blurring the authorizing signature and I entered the inspection gate certain I would be asked to leave the country on the next plane. I had so completely identified Indonesia as the super-anti-American country of the underdeveloped world that I would not have been surprised if I had been turned over to the police:

Especially during the past year, Indonesians had repeatedly attacked both public and private American enterprises all across the archipelago. In Djogjakarta, local officials closed the United States Information Service's Jefferson Library and declared it off-limits for the Americans in charge. Several thousand demonstrators raided the U.S. Consulate at Surabaja, tore up the American flag, and wrote the usual slogans on the walls—"Down with Yankee Imperialists," "*Ganyang* America," etc. *Ganyang* is Malay for "crush with the teeth." A youth group tore up the American Cultural Center in Djakarta. Several Indonesian post offices refused to accept U.S.I.S. mail. Garuda, Indonesia's domestic airline, refused U.S.I.S. air freight. The government harassed U.S. cultural performers, including my friend Tony Scott, the jazz clarinetist, who was arrested for "fraternization." A boycott against American films was effective in most big cities. A government order outlawed the Boy Scouts. Demonstrators marched against the rubber estates of Goodyear and U.S. Rubber and the government verged on a "protective takeover" of the properties. Airport workers twice refused to service U.S. passenger aircraft, forcing both planes to leave without unloading their passengers. A government decree forbade student visits to the United States. The National Youth Front attacked Peace Corps facilities in Medan, Kediri, Semarang, and Pakan Baru. Press, radio, TV, and other media, all government controlled, kept up a steady flow of anti-American reportage. And posters and banners at rallies and along main streets in the big cities endlessly repeated anti-American slogans, appropriately illustrated by caricatures

of Uncle Sam in his dollar-sign suit wielding rockets and bayo-
nets. Ultimately, Sukarno himself endorsed all this with scores of
anti-American references, both in public speeches and private
conversations. He also personally banned journalists representing the Luce publications and, with one exception, refused
private interviews for journalists from any Western country. . . .

The inspector read my soggy passport and asked me if it were
true, as written, that I was an American journalist. He seemed
ominously skeptical to me. I showed him the letter I carried from
the *Saturday Evening Post.* Forthwith, he stamped my visa without reading it. No one looked in my bags. And an armed guard
volunteered to carry them to a taxi. As it turned out, Sukarno had
decided to capitalize on the limelight focused on Indonesia by its
withdrawal from the United Nations. Not only customs inspec-
tors, but high government officials were instructed to make life as
easy as possible for foreign journalists.

In a way, this was a fair example of an important aspect of the
Indonesian-Malay temperament. Relaxed and easy-going, it con-
ceals an exceptional capacity for sudden and sometimes violent
turnabouts. *Amok* is a Malay word that describes extraordinarily
wild behavior by someone normally placid and predictable. I
must say, however, that I had no inkling then of the violent deeds
destined for October, 1965.

Djakarta is a crowded, crumbling city disguised by perpetually
green trees. Its three million people, mostly poor, live in low, old
buildings, mostly falling apart. There are not many people sleep-
ing in the streets. Djakarta is amorphous. It has no single downtown district but many market areas, each providing a hub for
community life. A great open sewage canal slices sluggishly
through the city, carrying away waste and providing bathing
facilities for the very poor. There are all sorts of gross new
monuments scattered about, especially in the area immediately
adjacent to the government complex. Most of them commemorate
a great moment in the long struggle against Dutch rule. Near the
city line, Russian funds have built a vast sporting complex.
And not far from Sukarno's Merdeka Palace, there is the new,

twelve-story Hotel Indonesia, where most foreign visitors stay in first-class accommodations far removed from the wretchedness of Djakarta. Everywhere in the city, tricycle pedicabs, horsecarts, and a surprising number of cars clog the streets. There are few buses, or at least not enough. It seems no bus can move in Djakarta without a dozen or so young men clinging to its sides. Pickpockets were said to thrive on unsuspecting foreigners who made the mistake of squeezing inside. But I rode often, with my hand on my wallet.

At the emotional center of all this is Merdeka Palace, where Sukarno lives. It looms up in disdainful white splendor, a memory of the power of Dutch governors. The name "Merdeka" means "freedom" and is only as old as Indonesian independence. But the look of the place is imperial and to live in it is to live like a king rather than the leader of an austere, go-it-alone revolution. It was in the shadow of the Palace, in the vast park just across the boulevard, that Sukarno, in May, 1964, had told a crowd of about a hundred thousand that he meant it when he said to the United States, "Go to hell with your aid."

Most days during my stay, dark-eyed students in white shirts and tight pants demonstrated within earshot of the palace. They carried signs that read GANYANG-MALAYSIA-INGRIS-AND-AMERICA! They also sang a nameless anti-Western song that has an interesting history. It had been introduced to the Indonesians during World War II by the conquering Japanese, whose seminal contributions to postwar antagonism toward the West in South Asia have scarcely been acknowledged. When the Japanese went away, most Indonesians stopped singing the song. It offended the gentle disposition of the average man. It was something of an insult to the memory of two million Indonesians killed or worked to death under the Japanese occupation. And since the United States had supported Indonesian nationalism, it did not exactly apply. But times changed. In the late fifties, the ubiquitous Communist Party (P.K.I.) revived the song and made it a hit among student demonstrators. Translated, the first stanza went:

Watch out for English and Americans
The enemy of all Asians
They commit the most heinous crimes
Toward the Asian people

And the chorus, sung to a lilting tune reminiscent of college days, was:

Smash them to pieces!

The first time I heard that song I was riding in a tricycle pedicab on my way to Merdeka Palace for my first meeting with Sukarno. It was my second day in Djakarta. I had left the hotel, passed what remained of the British Embassy, which had been recently burned out by rioters protesting the British presence in Malaysia, and was approaching Merdeka Barat. Here I came up behind about five thousand students milling about at the end of an anti-Western demonstration. They were shouting and shaking their fists, but one by one, they made way for my pedicab, always with a happy laugh: The pedicab was not my size, my knees were level with my chin, and rather than pedal my weight, the driver was pushing it. And when the congestion stalled all traffic, a student turned on me to ask for an autograph. As Eric Hoffer would understand, the Indonesians were going about "the sober, practical task of modernizing a backward country (by) the staging of a madhouse." The youth handed me a notebook and a pencil. I signed my name. He said he wanted most of all to visit and perhaps study in the United States. And when I asked him what the demonstration was all about, he launched into a detailed recitation.

"Protesting against you and the English," he said. "Some of us are against the whole system represented by the United States and want to build anti-American public opinion in Indonesia. Others are frustrated because, on many occasions, the policy or the statements of American officials, or press statements reporting events in Indonesia discredits *America*. For example, just the other day, we heard your Associated Press had identified Chaerul

Saleh—he is a deputy prime minister, you know—as an anti-communist.

"Now, nobody who really knows Saleh would deny that this is true. But to say it in America puts Saleh in a bad spot. The President wants unity—unity, above all—among all parties—nationalist, religious, and communist. One who is *anti*communist is against the President's policy, don't you see? So to say that about Saleh is to hurt the interests of the noncommunist group here that does not want this country to go communist. There have been many, many incidents like this, each of which frustrates many people. You drive us crazy."

But why participate in a rally with the procommunists?

"It is politics. We show unity and give support to President Sukarno's policy, don't you see?"

Then the singing began and the youth translated: "Watch out for the English and the Americans. . . ."

Half an hour later, my pedicab dropped me at the rear of Merdeka Palace. Tradesmen near the gate sold fruit and candy, and another man advertised himself as a straightener of nails. An army paratrooper, smartly dressed in a maroon beret, starched khakis, and shiny jump-boots guarded the entrance.

Inside, two grand old banyan trees and a scattering of bronze nudes dominated the palace gardens, which are enclosed at one end by a gazebo, on two sides by new State buildings and a handsome mosque (all built under the personal supervision of Sukarno, an erstwhile architect) and at the other end by the stately white mansion itself. On the front porch, prowling up and down a marble passageway among enormous colonnades and beneath half-a-dozen glittering chandeliers favored by songbirds, there were six Japanese merchants on a trade mission, several female paratroopers, some petty officials, and eight journalists from Germany, India, Italy, and the United States. Among the Americans were Jerry King of the New York *Times,* Bernard Krisher of *Newsweek* and Bernard Kalb of C.B.S. News who, as a reporter for the *Times,* had once been jailed in Djakarta for alleged violations of Indonesian security. A pretty paratrooper who wore Borneo campaign ribbons put my name on the waiting list. She said the President would entertain the press as a group. At the moment, he was in conference with his ministers.

There was hardly a portent in Djakarta, as the reporters kept telling one another, that did not read ominously. The Indian was most pessimistic, for he saw Indonesia's Malaysian confrontation as a diversion for a forthcoming Chinese attack on India. Sukarno, everyone agreed, had drifted almost too far toward Peking and might soon become the prisoner of the P.K.I. What should America do about that? We were backing the British in Malaysia, enabling them to play a role akin to our own in South Vietnam, aiming at a reasonable power balance in South Asia—someday. Beyond this, our policy was to hold on, maintain a presence, and hope for a diplomatic break in the threatening weather—that is, for *something* to change Sukarno's heart. The reporters seemed opposed to this static policy, but most were also resigned to the prospect of a communist-dominated Indonesia, if not in Sukarno's lifetime, then immediately thereafter. Clearly, doing nothing was not the *something* that the situation demanded. But practical alternatives were difficult to imagine. Sukarno, head of the fifth largest nation in the world, defied analysis.

He had created an image of himself that somehow embodied the Indonesians' idea of themselves. Emperor-politician, a man with four wives, playboy of the Eastern world, supreme commander of one of Asia's biggest armies, official Great Leader of the Revolution, Sukarno moved against a background full of complex characters—some living, some in prison, some dead—and fantastic scenes from Java to Bali, back to Sumatra, to Moscow, Peking, Washington, and various international fleshpots. At age sixty-three, he had arrived at a ripe age for a man of the tropics, and riper still for one with most of one kidney gone and the other troubled with pesky stones. He had recently been bothered by swollen feet and those reporters who had known him over the years said he had aged noticeably in the past twelve months. Gossip had it that neither Nasser nor Tito would ever again invite him to their respective capitals because of his gargantuan appetites. But his hold on his constituency—more than one hundred million strong—seemed palpable at every level of society. It could be sensed the moment one saw people really admiring his picture on the wall of Kemajoran Airport. His outdoor speeches attracted, held, and moved to tears, laughter, or mania hundreds of thousands of people at a time. His name, "Bung Karno," was known in remote villages that had never heard of Djakarta. He was real to people as only legends can be real. The people—nearly all of them, one had to assume—loved *him*, whatever they thought about his commands. And, presumably, he loved them, after a fashion—he told them that he *was* Indonesia. Out of charisma, force and, above all, words, he had spun a cloak to cover reality.

Nearly twenty years after independence, for example, Indonesia's socialist economy had no detailed plan for development. According to Sukarno, this was as it should be. He had vowed *not* to spend Indonesia's independence on economic development because, he had said, this would impair the political struggle that must go on against imperialism until something approaching a Great Society of the World was achieved. When that day arrived, Sukarno had written, the people would be "mentally liberated" from colonialism, and ready finally for the promotion of affluence. He wanted his people steeped in struggle in order that they might become militant "in the sense of being so far determined to prosecute the revolution of mankind that no material sacrifice (was) too great to make." If all this sounded like a mishmash of Leninist jargon and a subconscious effort to delay the challenge of development and a sheer love of struggle (the latter being the stuff of legendary heroes), Sukarno seemed to say, then so be it.

In any case, one reality of Indonesia was that the economy was a shambles. Inflation was indeed amok. The cost of living, as in Brazil and many other "developing" countries, had skyrocketed: two thousand per cent in six years. An American dollar on the black market was worth ten thousand rupiahs. The official tourist rate was 1 to 500. The management of the Hotel Indonesia, with official permission, offered three thousand rupiahs for a dollar. Djakarta school teachers earned 1,250 rupiahs per week. Workers were generally paid partly in commodities—rice, cooking oil, and fifteen other staples—to supplement cash incomes that were often less than one dollar a month. Also, land reform had bogged down because of poor administration, bribe-giving landlords and bribe-taking officials. The Malaysian crisis had pinched off trade with mighty Singapore contributing to a two hundred million-dollar decline in exports of copra, oil, rubber, tin, and other products.

Meanwhile, nearly three quarters of the people were still managing to live at subsistence levels in the rural villages. They suffered, as they always had, but they survived. And in the cities, even the poorest souls made out somehow—moonlighting, grubbing, belt-tightening, and sharing with more favored relatives and friends in accordance with the national Moslem tradition.

But the point was, Sukarno seemed to feel no compulsion to do much about it. He had denied that Indonesia faced great economic difficulties. "The Indonesian people are faring reasonably well," he would say. "Just compare us to India or some other countries." I had done that and, of course, Sukarno was not wrong. Yet, in India, both Nehru and Shastri had made strenuous efforts to lead and to plan some viable mix of economic ideas to make a bad situation better. Sukarno's notion that a people fared "reasonably well" because they could live off fruit trees (harvested as often as four times a year) promised disastrous consequences, sooner or later.

Another example of Sukarno's approach to reality was Indonesian politics. His political watchword had been "Unity in Diversity," the Indonesian motto echoing *E Pluribus Unum.* He had fought for it against the Dutch, against religious fanatics, and against rebellious colonels from his own army. From Sabang to Merauke, he had never grown tired of talking about "National Identity, National Identity, National Identity." And, as we waited on the porch of Merdeka Palace, if there was a sense of unity in Indonesia—sweeping across the nation's three thousand miles and three thousand inhabited islands—if sixty million Javanese could somehow get along under one flag with Sumatrans, Balinese, and the rest, then this was Sukarno's greatest achievement. But Sukarno achieved this by molding a mass that worshipped *him*, Bung Karno. It remained to be seen whether "Indonesia" survived him.

There were other accomplishments. A nationwide educational system had been established, with the remarkable result that, in about fifteen years, the literacy rate had climbed from five per cent at the time of independence to more than sixty per cent at the end of 1964. All newspapers, however, were under strict government control, so that the newly literate masses could read only official news.

Again, a legislative system had been set up by Sukarno through which he received counsel from the nation's political parties and representatives of religious, nationalist, labor, rural, and military groups. The counselors, however, did little more than counsel. When a policy was put to a vote, they could vote only with Sukarno. Their effect was to "legitimatize" his power in the name of "guided democracy." At the meeting of counselors, called to consider Sukarno's previously announced decision to withdraw from the United Nations, thirty-three three-minute speeches were given affirming it. Although it may be presumed that there were some men who opposed that decision, the counselor system allowed no "negative" commentaries. Again, who could say whether such a precarious system would survive Sukarno?

During the first decade of the republic, Indonesia had been faced with political chaos. Sukarno had no political party of his own and the army was split by dissension and scattered revolts. But in a characteristic expression of the way he has used power—and most significantly for Indonesia and the rest of us—Sukarno decided to utilize the small but militant Communist Party, headed by Dipa N. Aidit, as a counter-balancing force against the power represented by the Socialists, the Nationalists, the Moslems and—especially—the military. For the resulting spectacle he coined the word *Nasakom*, representing the unity of all forces in the country that should flow into him as president. The result was order—of a sort. But the recognition given to the communists enabled the P.K.I. to mushroom. Besides adding nearly three million members to its rolls, it built important secondary strength among union members and organized peasants.

Order in Indonesia in January, 1965, seemed to depend largely on the alacrity with which Sukarno adjusted his policies, both foreign and domestic, to those being advocated in the streets by P.K.I.-led crowds. The other parties then had no choice but to go along with Sukarno. Thus, as far back as 1961, when the P.K.I. originated the idea of crushing Malaysia, even before it became a state, the communists knew they could count on a broad base of public support. Sukarno embraced the idea two years later. In 1964, the P.K.I. inspired a peasants' revolt in Central Java directed against the Sukarno government's own land reform pro-gram—but Sukarno wound up endorsing the peasants. And, finally, in as much as the P.K.I. sponsored endless anti-American demonstrations across the country, Sukarno was less and less able to retain even those relationships between the United States and Indonesia that were in *his* own self-interest.

And so it had gone down to the wire—the image of Nasakom and national unity vs. bankruptcy and the reality of burgeoning communist power. Again and again, Sukarno had taken his policy from the P.K.I. when, presumably, as a nationalist and Moslem as well as a Marxist, he could not best them. In recent days, how-ever, when D. N. Aidit asked Sukarno to arm fifteen million peas-ants and workers for the Malaysian emergency (and later, perhaps, for combat with the Indonesian army), Sukarno had demurred, saying that he would arm the entire nation *if* the crisis came to that—or, in other words, no. It was on such thin reeds that hope for a noncommunist, nonaligned Indonesia rested at this time.

With all this in mind, I was standing near the door to the palace waiting room when D. N. Aidit emerged to talk to the reporters. The communist chief was a frail, whippet-eyed man, age forty-three, wearing a baggy suit and a gray silk tie. "There is no peaceful way to solve the Malaysian dispute," he said. "That is why I am asking the President to give arms and ammunition to five million organized workers and ten million peasants to defend Indonesia from Malaysia and the British." Aidit was relaxed and smiling as he spoke. Once he broke off in the middle of a sentence to ask Jerry King where he was from. And upon hearing the name of the New York *Times,* he said, "That's the paper that makes trouble for people in Indonesia."

There was some commotion behind Aidit. Then one of the lady paratroopers invited the press to follow her through the waiting room into a much larger room with marble floors, a fine maroon rug, two giant chandeliers, and a circle of upholstered chairs ranged around a low table. In one chair, under a painting of Indonesian guerrilla fighters sat Sukarno himself. He stood up to greet us. He was a stocky man of medium height with good shoulders, slim hips, and military carriage. He reminded me of a school chum, the one who could be knocked down but would not stay down. He looked strong. No doubt he enjoyed deference most of all. He had the face of a man whose kick had been power for a long time. The black, black widely spaced eyes, the flaring nostrils, stormy mouth, and pointed chin were all instruments which he had often played for maximum effect. He hid his baldness under his trademark, a dark brown *petji.* He wore a khaki army officer's uniform with eight rows of ribbons, two medals and the wings of both a flier and a paratrooper. An ebony and gold swagger stick jutted out from his armpit. According to legend, the stick was a powerful talisman, protecting him from assassination.

Standing nearby, there were seven Indonesian political leaders, including Aidit and Chalid, head of the Moslem's biggest party, and Hardi, vice-chairman of the Nationalist party. "Look," Sukarno said, "*Nasakom*—we are all getting along very well together. Right?" The seven leaders snapped their heads in agreement. Then Sukarno promised to escort the press on a tour of his palace as soon as this meeting ended. We returned once more to the porch. Rain fell softly on the palace lawn.

At 11:30 A.M., Sukarno sent for us again. The politicians had gone. An army colonel, doubling as his appointments secretary, and one of the lady paratroopers guarded his flanks. Sukarno seemed cheerful, even a little elated, as though our presence were reassuring to him. "Before we quit the United Nations," he said, "no one paid any attention to us. And now, look, everyone is here!"

Several reporters immediately asked their pet questions, but Sukarno had no intention of talking politics. He said he wanted to show us his palace and pointedly asked if the American television cameraman were ready: a kind of sequel to Jacqueline Kennedy's White House tour.

We followed Sukarno into a huge reception room, museum-like in scope and feeling, lavishly draped, carpeted, and furnished. On the walls hung fragments of his extensive collection of romantic, realistic canvases, the remainder of which were displayed in other rooms and at three other palaces maintained in equal elegance for his occasional pleasure outside the capital. His taste ran to scenes of combat, tranquil landscapes, and portraits of Sukarno. He was particularly fond of a landscape of Flores Island in eastern Indonesia. Of the dozen years he spent in Dutch prisons for revolutionary activity, he had passed five of them on this island. "It was there," he told us, "that I pondered the five basic points of the revolution—belief in God, sovereignty of the people, nationalism, internationalism, and social justice." Photographs were discreetly exhibited, too. The ones that caught my eye were a close-up of Mao Tse-tung and a color shot of Sukarno with John F. Kennedy. "I liked Kennedy," Sukarno said. "So far, he is the only American President who could talk with me and with whom I could talk. I know Johnson, but I have not yet a clear opinion of him." There were marble and bronze sculptures, wood carvings, and examples of Indonesian folk art on tables, in display cases, and tucked away in odd corners behind the furniture. Some were fine, I thought, and all were consistent with the representational paintings. It seemed that Sukarno did not own a single piece of abstract art. Holding up a small doll dressed in a Balinese costume, he said, "This is a product of an Indonesian small industry that I started." Standing beside a glass-encased wood sculpture of the Chinese goddess of mercy, he said, "This is more than one thousand years old, a gift to me on my last visit to Peking. It is one of my best things. But I have many things at the Indonesian Pavilion at the World's Fair. I have a great longing to go to the Fair in New York."

After twenty minutes in the state room, Sukarno led us into a somewhat smaller room with an open porch facing the inner palace gardens. Here he displayed a collection of gongs, a carved elephant tusk, and a tankful of tiny, exotic fish. "Some people say that looking at fish relaxes their nerves," he said, "but fish make me nervous. They are never quiet. Always moving. They do not calm me."

When he turned away from the fish, he saw that the rain continued. "It has been an unusual rainy season, causing bad floods in Djakarta," he said. "Some people believe it is caused by the atomic bomb." One was left to decide for himself whether Sukarno agreed.

He stepped off the porch and strolled thirty or forty paces through the rain to a guest house, one of the new buildings in the palace complex. At the same time, our ensemble added three palace guardsmen in maroon berets, another army officer, and a pretty girl naval cadet. Sukarno introduced us to the girl. "I know the name of every staff member at every Indonesian embassy in every capital of the world," he said. "But I am beginning to suffer 'time cretinism.' I am writing my autobiography and I cannot remember all the dates and places I need . . . My health is all right. I am never tired, but I am never not tired. At seven o'clock each morning, I am busy. The secret is finding pleasure in life. I take pleasure in work, in life, in fight! I do not fast for Ramadan because of my kidney stone. I drink two liters of water every day. So I am fine." Now another woman joined the group, a lawyer wearing a sarong and jacket. Sukarno chatted with her, then presented her to the cameraman. "The emancipation of women goes faster in Indonesia than in Europe," he said. "Faster than in communist countries. You see? You should come to Indonesia without a bias. It is a misconception to say that Sukarno is a dictator, that Sukarno hates the West. Am I not peaceful?" He held his palms up to show that he was empty of guile. Then he led us back through the rain toward the palace. On the way, we passed the statue of a bosomy nude and the exquisite small mosque he had built for his private worship. "The Moslems complain about the nude being so close to the mosque," he said, with a laugh.

Again on the front porch, Sukarno shook hands with each of us. He asked me how tall I was and then touched my chest, which was about eye level for him.

"Your wife comes to here?" he asked.

I said yes.

"She is pretty?"

"Yes, indeed."

"That is good."

And while he was laughing, I asked him if I might see him alone sometime soon.

"Oh, yes," he said. Then he called to his appointments secretary. "Put this man's name in the book!"

We made a date for the morning of January 18, a Monday five days hence.

It had been an ironic hour with Sukarno. While he led us through his palatial museum, Indonesian volunteers under his orders were working their way along the footpaths of the Malaysian jungle looking for real people to kill with real bullets. He was not a combination of Franklin Roosevelt and Clark Gable, as the United States Ambassador, Howard Jones, once said, but he did have a kind of nostalgic charm. Even though the United States was his favorite symbol of hated imperialism, his anti-American-ism differed from that of the communists. Weighing against ideology was a weakness he could not hide: his vanity. Among nine journalists, he had given most of his attention to Kalb, King, the C.B.S. TV cameraman, and me. This was not because of our charm, I felt, but because America was still the epitome of glamor for him, the goal and the standard of achievement. For better or worse, he wanted to be *known* in the United States. Just spell his name right!

Over the next few days, I ran into more surprises. Despite runaway inflation, you could buy a gallon of gasoline for about *sixteen* rupiahs. That meant nearly seven hundred gallons cost one dollar's worth of black market rupiahs! The government supported the price to insure national mobility, such as it was, but it also provided a major windfall for private car owners—that is, for the rich and powerful few. On an off-loading pier down at the port, I counted more than a hundred small Fiat cars worth at least fifteen million black market rupiahs each. One drove by the afternoon I stood talking to a strange man I had met in a bazaar street. On his back, he wore a complicated salesman's rig that displayed a selection of low-priced tin buckets and also served as his wardrobe. His razor and toothbrush stuck out from a glass secured to a little shelf on one side. He did not live over his store, but under it. "If it were not for the soft breezes," he grumbled, "we would break many car windows." He also told me he could not remember the name of America's new President, but he had greatly admired John F. Kennedy.

There was no aspect of Indonesian life untouched by ironies, including the Indonesians' antagonism toward the United States. I asked around among both Indonesian and American sociologists in Djakarta and found that there was little reliable data on what Indonesian masses knew or thought or felt about America. One survey, of limited value since it was limited to upper class youth, did report that more than fifty per cent of those questioned said the country they would most like to visit was the United States—and this after a decade of the most intense anti-U.S. propaganda effort. If the feelings of most Indonesians remained obscure, there was some reason to believe a residue of good-will persisted—mainly, I thought, because Indonesians felt pretty good about life in general. Three hundred years of Dutch rule had failed to sell them on the Puritan ethic. Sukarno's revolution might have been more successful if it hadn't. Moreover, Indonesians, like most men in anything less than the most extreme circumstances, had a limited capacity for ill-will. Thus, antagonism toward their four million local Chinese displaced much of the spite that might have been concentrated on the United States. In many ways, the overseas Chinese were the Jews of Indonesia, the scapegoat of community bigots and stereotyped as merchants and moneymen. In the late fifties, Sukarno had ordered thousands of Chinese businessmen in small towns and villages to sell out and move into the cities. It was an act of open racism slowed but not reversed by the diplomatic intervention of Red China itself. And it produced a long period of chilly relations between Djakarta and Peking. Then, as Sukarno drifted toward alignment with Mao Tsetung, Indonesia's Chinese had begun to relax. But at the same time, they came under increasing Red Chinese pressure to support the local communist strategy. And this, in turn, earned them more contempt from anticommunist Moslems who acted as a restraining influence on Sukarno himself in his relations with Red China and the United States.

The most interesting observations on the accumulation of ironies that had led to the present explosive situation came to me one balmy evening at the home of a man I shall call Dr. N. He was a high official in the Ministry of X who had agreed to talk to me given a promise that I would not mention his name or his bureau. He lived in a pleasant house with a big yard, and he asked me to sit with him outside on lawn chairs because, he feared, his house was bugged. He never spoke above a whisper. At times, his speech was cryptic, and once he said to me: "If your notebook falls into the wrong hands, I won't be here tomorrow." My first question was how did Indonesia get into this mess and he spoke for ninety minutes. This is the essence of what he said:

"October 16, 1964, was a turning point here. I believe you will find that October, 1964, was a turning point in world history, too, because that is the month that China exploded her first nuclear bomb. But, as I say, October 16, was the exact date for Indonesia. It was on that day that D.N. Aidit announced that Sukarno's Five Points would not be needed here after unity was achieved. Of course, he meant unity as imposed by the P.K.I. and, of course, the point he had in mind was point number one, belief in God. Until then, the communists had always said they embraced all five points, and they could argue that communism in Indonesia was different than communism in China or the Soviet Union where God is not permitted. But now, Aidit had revealed his true colors, perhaps motivated by the knowledge that China did, in fact, have the means to make atomic bombs.

"This caused a reaction among Indonesian noncommunists. We are a religious people. For the first time, we felt free to criticize the Indonesian Communist Party. It was also a turning point in our economic and political thought which I consider very important. Before, everyone was afraid or reluctant to criticize because of the spirit of *Nasakom*. Suddenly, there was an awareness of the real difference between the communist and the noncommunist view. People saw a threat to the Five Points.

"Since October 16, 1964, there has been a new game of politics. One had to think about choosing a side in the controversy. The noncommunists tried to organize and immediately got into trouble because they were facing a disciplined communist party. They did not have time to solidify their position and the group they had formed, the Sukarnoist party, was quickly repressed by Sukarno himself.

"Now see what happens. Aidit tastes victory. So he goes even further than the government. He identifies the outlawed noncommunists or nationalistic communists with other political philosophies that were previously discredited, especially those with a religious orientation. He therefore renders them impotent and creates a new kind of fear, one that we have not had before. It is a situation very bad for Sukarno because now fewer and fewer groups stand between a final confrontation between the Communist Party and the Indonesian Army, which is itself divided. Thus, the trend is increasingly toward a confrontation—with Sukarno as the prize. But not quite yet. This year, certainly, but not quite yet.

"I have been analyzing the situation. Why did we resign from the United Nations and face world opinion—and why, which should interest you, do we hate America?

"First, I think of the Indonesian Constitution, which is the basic legalism of our nation. When was it drafted? It was drafted in 1945 in a fascist period under Japanese occupation. The Japanese were still here when Sukarno brought together the men who would draft the Constitution. Read it. You will find it has strong, national socialist ideas not far from the Axis ideas of that time. The basis of this Constitution is fascism, which has been the prevailing philosophy of this nation ever since and has been stronger than new thinking—that is, stronger than the idea that peace is of crucial importance and that democracy and human rights are what all men want.

"Now we are caught. Our philosophy forces us to adopt measures that may have been all right in 1940, but not in 1965. We have now a kind of McCarthyism that makes people afraid to speak or organize. And we are on our way to the point reached by the Germans and the Japanese in 1940. Our Constitution, our philosophy forces us to repeat their mistakes. Remember that Japan resigned from the League of Nations contrary to world public opinion? Remember Japanese expansion—it is no different than our involvement first in West Irian, now in Malaysia. Our philosophy blinds us to the real problems like world peace. We think only about anticolonialism, which is an obsolete issue. There is no colonialism. Times have changed since 1940. There are new nations all over Asia and Africa. Things are moving. New problems are arising. And yet Indonesia is bound to obsolete issues by an obsolete instrument, our Constitution.

"Now, I have a second thought. So far, Sukarno has been the strongest figure in Indonesia because of his historical role. He is father of the country, almost a dictator. He can do what he wants. No one can challenge him. As in a feudal society, he is thought of as a king. He is allowed to say what he wants without limitation. People are very tolerant of such a man. He is President for life.

"But, the man is getting old. He *is* old in a country that considers sixty years a very long life. So everyone here is now thinking of the post-Sukarno period. The struggle between communists and noncommunists here is all about succession. We are living through the last days of a great king. This is what is behind the U.N. crisis, the Malaysian crisis, the anti-Americanism, and—above all—the movement toward isolationism. Americans think of anti-Americanism in simplistic terms, in terms of propaganda. If people are anti-American, you think there must be something wrong with your American propaganda. But there is something so much deeper. Ask Sukarno. He will tell you. We want to be alone, because we have a problem we must solve, a problem that we alone can solve: Who will succeed Sukarno?

"So we are in the process of isolating ourselves. In this period, we have gained only one friend, Red China, for a price that will be far greater than that asked by the United States.

"I shall explain. Our communist friends forget that the overseas Chinese in this country have been a problem for centuries. We have a social and economic race problem here that is the same as the race problem in America—except that the Indonesian Chinese have economic power and do not want to integrate. This is Mr. Aidit's mistake. He leans toward Peking and will continue to move us in this direction hoping, as we suffer military losses, that Indonesia will be absorbed as a satellite by China. But we do not like the Chinese. We are isolated. We are suffering. We are not getting arms. We are, in short, frustrated. So, I think, we will explode against the Chinese and then wipe out the communists.

"After that, we will turn ultra-Right. The Islamic groups will join the military and the nationalists to form an ultra Right socialist government.

"A slaughter is inevitable. But you must understand this—the situation is fundamentally domestic. Anti-American feeling is only a by-product of the crisis we have gotten ourselves into.

"You have come to Djakarta at a time when Sukarno, after sensational events, is thinking, what next? He knows he has lost many friends. He feels lonely. Like all dictators, he does not like to be lonely. He may panic. He may cry. He may retreat, even be friendly to the press. But all this is only temporary. The great slaughter is coming this year, 1965. It is all very sad."

Dr. N. quietly smoked a cigarette almost down to the end. He squirmed in his lawn chair and scratched himself under his shirt. The mosquitos had come out and were biting both of us unmercifully. As I got up to leave, I asked him what he thought the United States should do about all this.

"America can do nothing to influence this situation," he said. "It is one hundred per cent domestic. All the anti-American demonstrations are organized by the communists, but the feeling against you grows. We *want* to be alone. You, then, should be neutral, strictly neutral. You can only lose by getting involved. Think about that. Americans always talk about getting involved as though it were, by itself, the Good. Not getting involved is sometimes better."

"Responsibility means involvement to us," I said.

"Responsibility is not a fact, but a belief. What you are most responsible for is your sense of what is responsibility in a given situation. Sometimes retreat is the best way to make a gain."

Later that night at the Hotel Indonesia, I sat on the veranda with my friend Sharma, from New Delhi, who had described himself as a photojournalist. I say "described" because no photojournalist I have ever known possessed anything like Sharma's erudition. It is not that photographers lack intelligence, only that they are not good listeners. I suspect that something more than a photographer was hidden behind his camera. Looking back, I am impressed by an observation he made that night which was to be followed about eight months later by the communists' abortive coup of September 30, 1965. A thirty-eight-man delegation from Red China, all dressed in gray uniforms cut in the fashion set by Mao Tse-tung, had clustered about the nearby reception desk. They were checking-in to be on hand for the ceremonial opening of Garuda's new Djakarta-Canton air route, Saturday, January 16, 1965.

"They remind me," Sharma said, "of some Japanese I met a few months before Pearl Harbor."

That weekend, I drove down to Bogor, a summer resort town forty miles south of Djakarta in the foothills of the Puntjak mountains. Sukarno's favorite weekend palace is in Bogor. The road was narrow and crowded with peasants on foot or driving horse-carts. Ramajava, a hairy, prickly fruit that tastes like sweet, fresh apricots, were in season. As I climbed into the hills, the weather improved—it rained, but it did not steam.

I stayed at the home of Bill Palmer, a bubbly American suspected of C.I.A. contacts. Naturally, he said the charge was ridiculous. Palmer had earned his living in Indonesia as the sole distributor of American films. He stayed on despite the boycott and entertained like a summer matron in Westhampton. It was said that Sukarno liked him and for reasons of his own, protected him from the P.K.I. One reason may have been this: Palmer continued to arrange special showings for Sukarno of new U.S. movies.

Whatever his affiliations, Palmer spoke up for the hawks' line in Southeast Asia, beginning with the domino theory and ending with the proposition that bombs dropped on Hanoi would settle the communists' hash in Indonesia. He didn't say how we would get out of Vietnam once we were so deeply involved.

Sunday evening, there was a party at the palace in Bogor. Sukarno and his number two wife, Madame Hartini, had invited three hundred guests in honor of an Indonesian diplomat. They had carefully *not* invited the press corps, but one of Sukarno's aides had told me I would be welcome if I presented myself at the outer gate. Here at dusk, I met Bill Worthy, the Negro-American journalist whose passport had been revoked after he had defied the State Department ban on travel in China. Worthy said he was doing Southeast Asia for *Esquire* and the *Saturday Evening Post*. He was traveling now with his birth certificate and visas stamped on attached sheets of bond paper. Sukarno had invited Bill to the party and, as it turned out, we were the only reporters on hand.

Beyond the gate on two or three acres of lawn, hundreds of miniature deer, originally bred in Japan, grazed in contentment. Twin fountains projected delicate streams into the sky to meet the light rain coming down. A helicopter was parked to one side. And at the end of a long ribbon of road, a palace of white stone arose from a broad outer staircase which sprouted great colonnades topped by an elaborate cornice. It was Dutch colonial architecture with a passion for the monstrous.

Inside under a ceiling two-stories above, a great marble hall easily held the large number of guests. Waiting for Sukarno and honored visitors, some sat in high-backed, upholstered chairs, which lined both long sides of the hall three-deep. Others shuffled about looking at the Bogor segment of Sukarno's art collection. And one or another strolled through his bedroom—canopied bed, thick yellow carpet, framed nude in pastels—to what seemed to be the only toilet available. There was one towel. The men wore neat business suits or military uniforms. The women had draped themselves in ankle-length sarongs with short jackets or stoles. They exposed very little flesh but lots of line.

About seven-thirty P.M., Sukarno entered, trailed by an entourage of military men and diplomats, and their wives. Madame Hartini, in an orange batik sarong and jacket, walked at his left side. And Cindy and Joey Adams, the U.S. comic and author of numerous jokebooks, walked on his right. Sukarno had chosen Cindy as collaborator on his autobiography. They had been working on it for more than a year, following on a friendship begun in 1961 when Adams first performed in Djakarta as a member of a U.S.-sponsored show biz troupe. She was dark-haired, dressed in a white gown with big red polkadots and a matching, ruffled stole. Her husband wore a dark suit with a red handkerchief waving in the pocket. No one laughed. Instead, as Sukarno marched down the long hall, splendidly outfitted in a black petji, black, beribboned uniform, and black socks, there was sustained applause. Sukarno answered the ovation with smiles and waves of his ebony baton. I caught his eye. He seemed surprised to see me. Then he and the entourage took seats in rows of comfortable chairs that squared off the far end of the hall—all except Cindy and Joey who sat next to me.

For the next hour, Sukarno stood to address the guests in Indonesian on the attributes of the honored diplomat, Sudjarwo, who had once been Indonesia's U.N. Ambassador and was now on his way to establish full diplomatic relations with the Netherlands.

In my time in Djakarta, it was often said that the Dutch, like the British in many of their former colonies, had become the most popular of all foreigners among their ex-colonials—perhaps because less was expected of them. The Dutch were back in Indonesia—in oil, rubber, and spices, for example—regardless of ideological differences. I believed it was true, although my information was secondhand, that some of the returning Dutch had visualized the bonanza inherent in anti-American pressure against U.S.-owned oil, rubber, and spice companies. They could reasonably expect to share in the profits if the government were to take over American interests, then re-lease them to new (perhaps Dutch) management. It was no surprise, then, that elements among the Dutch increasingly and ever more self-righteously spoke out against the American presence in Indonesia. Nor was it any wonder that they found a sympathetic audience—many Indonesians, after nearly two decades of "freedom", had begun to look upon the colonial period as "the good old days." But Dutch anti-Americanism astonished me; "anti-West" and "anti-American" were not interchangeable terms.

After his long speech, Sukarno accepted another round of applause with just a whiff of the matador in his bearing. Then he invited his guests to a buffet supper on the covered veranda in the west wing of the palace. We surrounded two long tables groaning under steaming platters of rice, fish, and vegetables, and soon picked them clean. An attendant told me I was to eat in an adjoining room with Sukarno and his entourage. I carried my plate inside, where Sukarno waved me to a nearby seat, next to Joey Adams. "You will dance tonight, Mr. Morgan," Sukarno said and I did not know whether that was a threat or a promise. Joey explained to me that Sukarno loved entertainment. "All his guards are entertainers," he said. "Every guest is expected to sing a song or say a few words on command. He's that kind of a man. I love him! He'd rather have a banana to eat and a pat on the hand than a million dollars and insults from the press. He is not an enemy of democracy. You would have to understand Indonesian politics to understand that. He's really a great guy. . . . He just insisted Cindy do his autobiography. All the time giving gifts—cuff links, *rugs*. In New York, we've got a houseful of stuff he's given us. And I give him things. I buy all his socks and shirts for him at Saks Fifth Avenue. . . . Get to know him. He's human. I love the guy!"

Meanwhile, I was reviewing all of the cautious criticisms of Sukarno that I had been listening to that week: Ruefully reflecting on Communist control of Antara, the government-owned Indonesian news agency, and on the widespread suppression of books, academic publications, and even open conversation, one critic had said, "I'm afraid Indonesia is ready for a revolution, but not for freedom." Another said Sukarno's revolutionary rhetoric, which emphasized political goals over economic progress, "simply means that Sukarno has no executive competence" in the development field. A third attacked him for failure to groom a successor. Neither Subandrio, the Peking-bent Foreign Minister; Saleh, the millionaire Third Deputy Prime Minister; nor Nasution, the ascetic Minister of Defense, seemed competent, even though they were most often mentioned in speculation about the post-Sukarno era. "Sukarno is like a father who won't let his sons grow up," one source observed and predicted that his real successor would be *chaos*. Sukarno had his priorities upside down.

Getting to know him, I thought his Marxism owed more of a debt to Groucho than to Karl—except that people were dying of it.

About 9:30 that night back in the main hall, Sukarno called for his entertainers. A seven-piece band, featuring a guitarist and a pianist, arranged itself in a circle at the open end of the room and struck up a number written by Sukarno, who "volunteered" the new ambassador to the Netherlands as first soloist. The man had no voice, but he chirped a few bars, off beat and out of tune. Then Sukarno himself crossed the hall in stockinged feet. He excused Ambassador Sudjarwo and sang the song as written. Over and over, the band repeated the chorus, providing rhythm for an approved two-step known as the *lenso*.

Sukarno briefly danced with Madame Hartini. Then, after assigning *me* to dance with her, he padded around the room appointing dancing partners for each of the ladies. Madame Hartini was a tall, handsome woman who bore herself with a kind of emphatic dignity. With a minimum of words, she taught me the *lenso* without taking her eyes off the air space above my left shoulder. I was an awkward pupil, but I learned. Then Sukarno returned, exchanging Madame Hartini for his twenty-year-old niece, who was shorter and less striking than her aunt, but more talkative.

"*Lenso?*" I asked.

"Yes—no Twist," she said.

"Is it illegal?"

She smiled. "Sometimes, I visit at the home of friends who want to Twist. We close the doors and shutter the windows, and do the Twist. But not here. My uncle says it is immodest and—American!"

After the dance, an Indonesian comedian billing himself as the Joey Adams of Djakarta told a string of jokes. Then D. N. Aidit, under orders from Sukarno, sang a roundelay. His voice was shy and reedy, but all the guests applauded as though their lives depended on it. After this, the dancing began again. This time my partner was a muscular young lady in maroon batik. I recognized her as one of the paratroopers I had met earlier in the week. She told me she had been the first guerrilla fighter dropped into Borneo.

"Now I'm studying journalism," she said.

At Merdeka Palace in Djakarta next morning at nine, Sukarno and I sat alone at the round table in his reception room. Beside the massive painting of Indonesian guerrilla fighters, there was an easel holding a portrait of Sukarno, dated Independence Day, August 17, 1945. In the portrait, he wore a uniform without ribbons and looked very dashing. This morning, he was in khaki, with the ribbons, and the *petji*, smoking English cigarettes. He still had dash—the cut of his lapels, the well-fitting shirt and neat tie, all worked for a striking effect. In those clothes, the emperor looked a hero born, fully capable of courting disaster and evading its consequences. The whole pattern of his life had been just this. He was a man fatally intrigued by his own prowess, in love as in politics. He was a Don Juan with one of the largest military forces in Asia.

Yet, it was necessary to distinguish between his exaggerated and florid style and the revolution for which he stood. He was an Indonesian. He was an Asian. He lived in an underdeveloped country, prone to extremes of passivity and anger. Even his Indonesian critics accepted his assessment of their general condition and regretted most of all that the West had so often discounted his opinions as propaganda. Granted that their lifetime President and Prime Minister—supreme commander of the armed forces and official Great Leader of the Revolution—was a vain, blustering, womanizing authoritarian with a crisis-loving mentality, an extreme taste for pomp and military circumstance, and too heavy a reliance on his skill as a spellbinding orator. But he was still the liberator, the unifier, of the fifth largest country in the world. He was *Bung Karno* embodying the God-like quality of "nation-building." And when he spoke in this role, he did indeed express some of their deeply-held feelings. Rightly handled, these feelings might even provide the necessary energy for the long pull in Southeast Asia.

Sukarno had often articulated a belief—he called it "my own definition"—that the world was made up of two blocs, the one that dominated and the one that wanted change. He called the first bloc "Oldefos," the old established forces. The second bloc was "Nefos," the new emerging forces. Shamelessly, he included the Soviet Union among the "Nefos" and left the status of Japan in doubt. But behind the jargon was a vision appealing to great masses in Asia, Africa, and Latin America. Largely because of world trade conditions and the problem of manpower, the *have* and the *have-not* nations were growing farther and farther apart. And with characteristic imprecision, Sukarno was probing the gap.

Sukarno offered me a cigarette, took one for himself, and struck a match for both of us. He said he had greatly enjoyed the party. I was to be complimented for my *lenso*. "I like Americans," he said, "but sometimes I dislike American policy. American policy does not understand the twentieth century." According to him, the twentieth century had to do, first of all, with the creation of independent nations in Africa and Asia including, of course, Indonesia. "You do not understand," he said, "that the twentieth century is the period in history of Asian-African nationalism." Nationalism, he explained, is essentially a desire for freedom and independence. "I value the four freedoms of Mr. Roosevelt very much," he said, "but I have added freedom number five, that is, the freedom to be free. The United States has often intervened in the freedom of new nations to be free." He cited the example of C.I.A. intervention in Indonesia in 1958, when America supported the Sumatran rebellion against Sukarno. Our involvement was climaxed by the shooting down and capture of a "civilian" pilot named Allen Lawrence Pope after he had bombarded an Indonesian airfield from an old B-25. "We shot down his plane," Sukarno said, "and captured Lawrence Pope, American. We sentenced him to death, but later I pardoned him because I did not want to spoil the good relationship between Indonesia and America by executing Lawrence Pope, American." Sukarno did not mention the ransom he had received for Pope's freedom. He said bombing Indonesia was the sort of thing he didn't like.

He removed his *petji* and stroked his bald crown. Then he replaced the *petji*. He insisted there was no basic anti-Americanism in Indonesia. "What there is," he said, "is dislike for intervention. We want to be free. To be completely free. We want to be left alone." But not completely alone. Sukarno condemned President Johnson for sending an American military consultant to Malaysia. "Why should Johnson do that?" he asked. Yet he was not averse to American intervention in the Malaysia crisis on his own terms. "Why doesn't President Johnson urge the Prime Minister of Malaysia to have a peaceful solution with Indonesia?" he asked, disingenuously. Then Sukarno intoned his case against Malaysia, questioning the "self-determination" procedures used in establishing the new state in 1963, and accusing the British of "neo-colonialism." But did this justify an invasion or the one billion dollars a year spent by Indonesia on armaments?

Was he an old-fashioned expansionist? "It is not my policy," Sukarno said, "to make Indonesia a dominating force in Southeast Asia. My policy is to make Indonesia strong, as a state and as a nation. If by our number, one hundred four million now, and by our strategic position, economically, socially, and politically, if Indonesia becomes a dominating factor in Southeast Asian life, that is quite understandable, but not my aim."

Was he looking for an excuse to align himself with the communist bloc, especially Red China? "My policy," Sukarno said, "is Asian-African unity. Even more than that, it is combined action of *all* new emerging forces. This has nothing to do with communist China except in so far as it is a new emerging force. There are new emerging forces in America, too. It is my own definition and analysis that the Indonesian revolution is only part of the great revolution of mankind."

Was he contriving the classic method of "exporting" economic discontent? "But we are not facing great economic difficulties," he said. "We have a new variety of rice just developed that will give twice as much production as normal rice. It is quite an achievement from our own research center. I wrote a poem about it, I was so happy. But it is untranslatable."

Was he seeking isolation in order to "build the nation"? Sukarno shook his head. "My point is not to withdraw Indonesia from the turmoil of the world," he said. "I want Indonesia *in* the relationships of the world. I hope the interest is growing."

Nothing shook Sukarno's insistence on the purity of his motives. Further questioning seemed useless, so, instead, I suggested that he consider the effect of Indonesian antagonism toward the United States on *us*. I said the politics of anti-Americanism might result in more rather than less U.S. intervention. But Sukarno denied that such a "politics" existed. "Absolutely not," he said. "What we are doing is regretting that American policy is so bad towards Asia and Africa. Our feelings are not antagonistic. They are *re-active*. Indonesia does not like American policy here and elsewhere. This is not basic antagonism. I hope that America at long last sees the mistake it is committing."

Sukarno's appointment secretary abruptly came into the room by a rear door. I found myself wondering what I would have done were he an assassin. It seemed my time was up. What, I asked, about our U.S.I.S. libraries? Sukarno came forward and, palms down, placed his thick-veined hands on the table. He said he had told U.S. Ambassador Howard Jones that the library-burnings and other incidents all reflected a prevailing dislike of U.S. policy. "We are living in a period of solidarity among new emerging forces," he said. "Now what happens in other parts of Asia and Africa affects us also. What the Asians and Africans feel, we feel, too. What American policy does in Asian and African countries, we feel, also. This makes a widespread feeling of dislike all over Asia and Africa. And as a result of this come demonstrations against American libraries."

Sukarno arose, looking down on me as though I might never understand. "We Indonesians were angry and felt insulted by the American Senator who, after the burning of books in the American library in Djakarta, scolded us for being uncivilized because we burnt books. That man could not understand that this was an explosion of dislike for American policy. Moreover, what was burnt was not the books, but the spirit of the books. What would that Senator say about the burning of books by Martin Luther? Was *he* uncivilized? I am not defending Protestantism, understand. And I am not defending the act of burning U.S.I.S. books. I deplore the burning of those books. But I also understand the motives of those students who burn the books."

Sukarno waited for me to rise. Then he took my arm and walked me to the porch. In the park across Merdeka Barat, there was a memorial obelisk, with a light tower on top, but no lights. Sukarno forbade this finishing touch after a seer had predicted he would die the day the lights went on. Sukarno said he was very proud of the obelisk. Then at the head of the stairs, he shook my

hand. "Movies, too," Sukarno said. "We boycott them because we dislike American policy. And, I must say candidly, there are some American movies that, indeed, hurt the feelings of the brown and the black man. Several years ago, I had a talk with my friend, Eric Johnston, chairman of the American motion pictures association. I like him. I said, 'Please, Eric, don't make any more pictures that hurt our feelings.' I spoke to him about an American picture, *The Broken Arrow*, a love story between an American officer and an Indian squaw-girl. Why should that picture hurt the feelings of Indians? Why should at the very last minute the squaw-girl have to die? I suggested to Eric Johnston, next time make a picture that ends happily. Let them live happily ever after."

Next day, through a literary agent in New York, an editor of *Life* magazine, one of the Luce publications banned in Indonesia, asked me to cable a piece about the political atmosphere in Djakarta. I said I would if *Life*, for which I had never worked, would promise not to publish an edited version of my article without my approval and if I were free to advise Sukarno of the assignment. Acceptance of both these conditions required two cable phone calls and three cablegrams. Then I began working on the piece while trying to arrange a second interview with Sukarno. I felt I owed it to him to let him know that his answers to my questions would soon appear in *Life*. But I could hardly explain this to his appointments secretary. So I sent a note to the palace saying I wanted to ask a few more questions to clear up several conflicting points that had been made. And again I was impressed by Sukarno's momentary availablity. The appointments secretary phoned to say that the President had made room for me on his Friday calendar by delaying a State meeting.

When Sukarno and I were alone once again, he seemed to know what was on my mind. I said I had something to tell him he might not like. He smiled and looked up at a finely carved molding. I described the calls and cables from New York, assuring him that I had not come to Djakarta on false pretenses. Sukarno nodded and lit one of his English cigarettes. I had visions

of a sinister intelligence officer monitoring my phone at the Hotel Indonesia and reading my cables before delivery. Finally, I said I had a few more questions to ask (none very important) if he still did not mind talking to me. Sukarno's eyes rolled up. He blinked. Had he been listening to me?

"What is your first question?" he asked.

It dawned that he might have been daydreaming all this time and that he not only did not know about the *Life* assignment, but really did not care. We were both part of a tired game in a Kiplingesque world, rewritten for Pax Americana. He represented the power of a state and I identified with the power of my own state in a world that made us both more than a little paranoid— and me, increasingly so as I traveled and the problems loomed larger and harder to define. More and more, I recognized the symptoms in myself, the desire to escape confusion, the yearning for a simple conception, the growing willingness to go it alone and to rely on force, rationalized as responsibility. I wanted to get the hell out of Indonesia.

5
Egyptians

There were ten days in Singapore that I spent mostly working on the *Life* article and eating what must be the best Chinese food in the world. I wrote in a cautionary spirit, less self-righteously indignant about old Sukarno than anything *Life* had ever published. But Sukarno, as I learned later, hated my article more than most and even denounced me in an address in the Djakarta sports arena. He had to preserve his image.

From Singapore, I flew on over India and Saudi Arabia to Cairo. I landed on the morning of February 6, during a period of increasing hostility toward Israel, and its corollary, anti-Americanism. As our former Ambassador to Egypt, John S. Badeau, had just written in *Foreign Affairs,* "a crisis in confidence" threatened U.S.-U.A.R. relations. Badeau, who was at pains to justify the Kennedy policy of "selective cooperation" with Egypt which he, Badeau, had represented, listed three counts against America that contributed to Egyptian suspicion and distrust in the Johnson era. One was the "unpredictability" of our policy since the 1952 Revolution. Another was the rise of our power, "particularly in and near the Middle East." And the third was "our association with the British and the 'reactionary' Arab regimes"—in Egyptian terms, we were among the forces of "imperialism and neocolonialism." All three counts, moreover, were aggravated by the Israeli problem, which prompted the Egyptian belief "that Israel exercises a veto power on American policy toward the Arab world." It seemed a good, angry time to be in Cairo.

Looking forward to my visit, I had assumed that I, as a Jewish-American journalist, might be subject to all sorts of special inquiries and delays in Egypt. So, in New York, I wrote "Protestant" on my Egyptian visa application. I felt a fraud when I did it, and more so at Cairo airport. Riding the limousine into the city, I gave a squeeze to the tiny *mazuzah* on my key ring, but it was small comfort.

My first impression of the Egyptians (filtered through my guilt feelings) depended, as first impressions in new places often do, on the limousine's route into town. We had followed a broad parkway, turned off, doubled back, and entered a splendid residential section. Town houses in the British style and several expensive-looking apartment buildings lined the streets. An occasional air-conditioner looked out from upper windows. There were neat gardens and lush trees, zealous sweepers and uniformed nannies, natty cops and late-model cars. It was Bronxville, for people who are more equal than others. I suspected the route had been planned by a Chamber of Commerce man who understood about first impressions. Of course, I might have been wrong, but during my three-week stay, I never got over the sense that the authorities wanted their foreign visitors to see, first of all, how elegant bourgeois Cairo remained thirteen years after independence.

Likewise, Egyptians were always telling me that they ran the Suez Canal more efficiently than the British ever did. And they were right. It was the urgency with which they pressed the point that seemed to confirm the suspicions of my first moments in Cairo: they were a people with a particularly well-developed inferiority complex.

I had passed through Cairo twice before, but this was my first real visit. It is an Arab-English-French city of three million people in love with a river. The Nile flows through the heart of town,

setting the pace for the life it makes possible. People adore it.
And you could understand why so many great religions began
with only an oasis. Water is a miracle to a man in a desert.
During the post-revolution Dulles-honeymoon with Naguib and
Nasser, American aid helped beautify walks, gardens, bridges,
and boat landings along the Nile. Many Egyptians who resent
our wheat shipments and our attitude toward Israel still grate-
fully remember us for that. I stayed at the Nile Hilton. It had
been constructed at one end of a line of British-built (and, I was
told, better-run) hotels looking across the river toward a small
island where fragile gardens formed a backdrop for a pleasant
open-air cafe. For reasons known only to the State, someone had
erected an absurd tower, 630 meters high, in the center of the
island, effectively spoiling Hilton's view of the pyramids on the
western horizon. Once I spent a day taking the four-dollar tour of
the Sphinx and those man-made mountains in Giza. They are the
world's outstanding symbol of eternal "camp." The side streets of
Cairo are a potted maze and the slums of "Old Cairo" can be
matched with the worst *favela*. Moreover, there was a desert
wind, the *khamseen*, that blew for several days, blotting out the
sun and reminding you that thirty million Egyptians live in a
country that is ninety-five per cent sand. In 1970, the Russian-
financed Aswan Dam would add perhaps two million acres of
land to the paltry total—a help, but no salvation. By 1980, Egypt's
population would be fifty-four million still confined to the narrow
green banks of the Nile. Yet with all this, there was Cairo's colos-
sal joke: the old, bearded men in flowing desert robes, the dark-
eyed lads in pajamas, the chic young women wearing uplifts and
mesh stockings, the serious business types in dark glasses, and
Nasser himself, whose photograph beams at you from store windows and billboards all over the city—everyone, in fact—looked
Jewish. I often sat for an hour at a time in Liberation Square, the
great mall outside the Museum of Egyptian Civilization, just
watching the kids play ball, the vendors hawking their hair combs
and ballpoint pens, and the worthies on their knees praying East,
asking myself how come I had never known we were all related.

Once I even suggested to a representative of the Arab League that Egypt ought to form a common market with Israel looking toward a united Semitic nation in the Middle East. "Look what the French and Germans have done," I said. The man was struck dumb.

Funny things happened to me in Cairo. In my room one afternoon, I was stretched out in my undershorts trying to work my way through Herman Finer's book, *Dulles Over Suez*, which I had carried halfway around the world. It is a passionate indictment of Dulles' failure to support England, France, and Israel in the Suez-Sinai war of 1956 when, he maintains, the Soviet Union might have been faced down and Nasser overthrown. Finer would have favored a 1962 Cuban-style eyeball-to-eyeball confrontation with the Russians in the Middle East to achieve "this puncturing of the Soviet balloon . . . six years earlier." Under the circumstances, Finer argues, the risk of World War III would have been acceptable. Finer also believes that our own interests plus our moral obligations toward civilization were compelling reasons for toppling Nasser, "well known to be a desperado." Yet *this* assumed Nasser would not be succeeded by an even more desperate man driven to even greater extremes by popular demands for vengeance and retribution. I was finding Finer's purple vehemence as unconvincing as Dulles' own rationalizations when a hotel clerk phoned. He said I had received a registered package for which I must sign at the desk. I pulled on some clothes, fished around for my room key among the usual pocket-paraphernalia I had piled on my dresser, and dashed to the elevator. I signed for my package (my wife had sent some medicine) and rode up again. My door was locked, but as I dropped my key on the dresser, I realized my *mazuzah* and its key ring were gone. It seemed nothing else had been touched, although *Dulles Over Suez* rested on an end table; I thought I had left it on the bed, but I could not be sure.

It was a lovely little *mazuzah*, blue metal trimmed in gold with tiny decorative stones inlaid at the top. My friend John A. Williams, the author of *Night Song* and several other good books, bought it in Israel and gave it to me just before I left New York.

A maid or a bellhop might have swiped it, thinking the inexpensive stones were actually precious. But then, why hadn't she or he taken the money crumpled up on my dresser? Or my air tickets? I decided I had been investigated by the Egyptian F.B.I. or SMERSH—and expected, at any moment, to be exposed and denounced as a Jewish spy traveling on a fraudulent visa application. It was too late, obviously, to make a break for the U.S. Embassy (a close three blocks away, and yet so far!) or to learn Karate: I had once chopped unsuccessfully at a piece of wood with the side of my palm, which was sore for days after. So, I made the only move possible under the circumstances. I grabbed my wallet, dashed to the first-floor gift shop, and purchased a new key ring and pendant engraved with an Egyptian lotus symbol. Then I bought and attached a small pen knife, and returned to my room for rehearsals:

"Is this yours, M. Morgan?" *they* would ask.

"What is that?" I would reply, interested but calm.

"That is a key ring with a *mazuzah* attached."

"A *mazuzah?*"

"A symbol, M. Morgan, a Jewish symbol."

"Oh, no," I would say. "I have my own key ring. No keys, of course. Ha ha. Don't need keys in Cairo. Just a pen knife for cutting string. And this pendant. Egyptian lotus for good luck. Ha ha. It's the symbol of staying alive. . . ."

The knock on the door never came, however, and I relaxed. Perhaps I had been robbed. But I wanted to believe I had somehow outwitted *them.*

Another afternoon, another moment: I looked up the phone number of the Middle Eastern Feature Service, a news syndicate that employed Zein Navatny, a sometime special assignment reporter for the New York *Times.* A *Times'* friend had given me his name to call for background on attitudes toward the United States in the Arab world. Four times I called Zein's number and four times I received either a wrong number or a busy signal. At last, I asked the hotel operator to recheck the number and place the call for me. Moments later, she called me back.

"There's your Mr. Zein," she said.

"Hello, Zein?" I cried.

"Yes, who is there?" Zein asked.

"Morgan! Your name—I got it from friends at the New York *Times*."

"Oh, that is fine. How is New York?"

"New York is fine, Zein. May I buy you a drink this evening?"

"Why not? Seven o'clock at your hotel?"

"Fine, Zein."

"Good. I look forward, Morgan."

He was a tall Lebanese wearing an expensive black pin-striped suit and dark glasses. His collar was fastened with a gold clip. His tie was black with black figures. He wore French cuffs linked by ebony buttons. Being permanently rumpled myself and having known few working journalists who were not, I was startled by Zein's get-up. But we settled down in the Hilton cocktail lounge and talked pleasantly over our first martini. I told him about Djakarta. He told me about Socony Mobil, the U.S. oil company, for whom he had once worked. I told him about a mutual friend at the New York *Times*. He told me about a serious problem of airport clearance for Middle East Airlines.

It dawned on me that whoever this man was and whatever his name, he was not my *Zein Navatny*.

"Say, Zein," I said, "have you got a card?"

"Sure, Morgan," he replied.

We exchanged cards. His name was *Chasic Zein*. He managed Middle East Airlines, whose number is just above Middle Eastern Feature Service in the Cairo telephone book.

"Thank you," I said.

"As I was saying," Zein continued, "the Arab world is not monolithic except in regard to the question of Israel. But I feel a whole generation of Arabs has been disillusioned by American idealism. It began when John Foster Dulles refused Nasser money for the Aswan Dam. This created the necessity for taking over the Suez Canal—for *show*—which began the Suez crisis, and brought in Soviet aid to build Aswan, and started the whole trend toward the East here. In our hearts, we still yearn for America. But we are going the other way."

"But Egypt bought arms from Russia in 1955 before the decision on the dam," I protested.

"Because we could not buy arms from *you!* We expected America to be the arbiter, the leader in the Middle East. Instead, you sided with Israel."

"Only to maintain a balance here."

"No, that is not right. There is no balance. The Arabs fear Israel's know-how. Arabs are humiliated by Israel's progress. This has caused upheavals in many Arab governments. I wish I understood what made Dulles behave the way he did—"

Chasic Zein suddenly understood one thing: that he and I had not been destined to meet. Something I did or said, some sudden realization that our conversation at the Nile Hilton over martinis was too unlikely—somehow he understood and wanted to escape. He did not know who I was, only that a mistake had been made. Or a trap set! Chasic Zein began to perspire. Then politely, but abruptly, he excused himself. I kept his card, but I did not see him again.

I missed the real Zein Navatny, too. He was in Yemen, I was told. But he might have been elsewhere. You never know.

One Saturday morning after I had been in Cairo talking to people for a week or so, I finally got around to the United States' Embassy compound to see what was left of the John F. Kennedy Memorial Library. On Thanksgiving Day just past, a mob of two hundred Congolese students and a few Egyptians had attacked the compound and set fire to the library. Nearly thirty thousand books valued at two hundred and fifty thousand dollars were destroyed. Shouting slogans against American "imperialist aggression" in the Congo, the mob seemed to be swept along by the worldwide wave of anti-U.S. demonstrations touched off the day after American and Belgian paratroops descended on Stanleyville to rescue the Congolese rebels' foreign hostages. But hostility toward us had been building in Cairo since midsummer over the full range of East-West issues (Vietnam, Cyprus, Israel, Cuba, the Congo). And two days before Christmas, rather like Sukarno, Nasser added to it in a speech suggesting Americans could "drink from the sea" if they did not like Egyptian behavior. The American equivalent of that phrase is "go jump in the lake." Ever since, the government-controlled Cairo press had kept up the assault on almost every facet of U.S. foreign policy. Now, almost three months after Thanksgiving, the twenty-year-old orange stucco, two-story library, which had only recently been dedicated to the memory of J.F.K., remained a bleak symbol of this atmosphere. Restoration work had not begun. The façade was charred and smoke-stained. And slabs of wood covered the windows, each like a patch over a blind eye. For a while, I stood on the street looking up at it. I felt cold even though the sun streamed through the trees. Then I noticed a dozen or so Egyptian soldiers lounging at the head of the street about one hundred yards from the compound's side gate. They carried long, metal-tipped riot sticks, which are almost as efficient crowd-dispersers as guns. They were on guard against any new attack on the U.S. compound, but the damage had been done.

Much of the anti-American sentiment could be traced to a visit from Nikita Khrushchev in May, 1964. Nasser was still maintaining that atheistic communism was antithetical to God-fearing Egyptian socialism. But for Khrushchev's benefit he pardoned several hundred communists serving time in detention camps and allowed the journalists among them to take jobs on various Cairo newspapers, all of which are government-controlled. Khaled Mohieddin, who had been among the small group of "Free Officers" responsible for the 1952 coup and whose communist sympathies later landed him in jail, was named editor of Cairo's largest-circulation paper, *Al Akhbar*. Another communist took over as head of a weekly magazine and still others were placed in positions of influence on the staff of *Al Ahram*, Egypt's most influential daily, edited by Mohammed Hassenein Heikal, one of Nasser's closest friends. By the time Khrushchev departed, a move to the left in Egyptian affairs was marked and especially noticeable in the newspapers. *Al Ahram* moved more slowly than the rest but it, too, began to increase its coverage of Soviet news and its emphasis on unflattering pieces about the United States.

In early August, for example, twelve issues of *Al Ahram* carried seven articles reflecting the new mood. Three attacked the C.I.A., one interpreted Vietnam as American aggression, one reported on Castro's latest criticism of the U.S., and two praised the Republican Presidential candidate, Barry Goldwater, because he was opposed by U.S. Jews. One of the latter regretted that Goldwater was not America.

There were other signs of change. Increasing numbers of trade missions set off from Cairo for Eastern European countries. The Russians enlarged their economic commitments, in exchange for which Egyptian leaders made repeated public professions of undying friendship for the Soviet Union. Finally, Nasser was threatening to recognize East Germany's communist regime, ostensibly to punish West Germany for transshipping U.S. arms to Israel, but well aware that both East and West would interpret such a move as a gesture of alignment with the Soviet bloc. Under these circumstances, it was predictable that Egyptian attitudes toward the United States would increasingly reflect ideological differences rather than material conflicts subject to negotiation. We had our ideology. They had theirs which, as time passed, was becoming a mirror of Soviet ideology.

But what was happening to bring about change now? After a decade of the most consummate juggling between the great powers, resulting in steady gains for Egypt's economy and its self-esteem, Nasser seemed about to give up his "neutral" role and throw in his lot entirely with the Russians. He risked losing not only U.S. surplus food worth more than one hundred million dollars in 1964, but also the West's credit that supported well over half of the national development programs. Why?

One could speculate: Even with American aid, a serious food and financial crisis was at hand. By establishing his independence of the United States, Nasser would have a ready made straw man when the shortages came. He would enhance his own prestige by taking a stand against America on "principle" and, at the same time, he would be able to say the nation starved because it would not submit to American pressure in Yemen, on the Israeli border, and in the Congo where he had been sending arms for the rebels. Given the makings of anti-Americanism—our power, our support of Israel, our alliance with the old colonial powers, and our ambivalence—Nasser could shape a political issue strong enough to maintain himself in power. He had always justified his foreign adventures in terms of national prestige that warranted money and food from both East and West. Now, like Sukarno, he would ride on the back of the nearest communist tiger. It remained to be seen whether he wound up inside.

But it wasn't that simple. Even as I brooded about our burned-out library, Nasser was appealing for thirty-five million dollars in U.S. surplus commodities. And even though East German Premier Walter Ulbricht was on his way to Cairo for a visit, Nasser and his controlled press were rather carefully concentrating their anti-Western antagonism on West Germany.

Time and again, those I met wanted to make sure I understood the *difference* between anti-American feelings in Egypt and elsewhere among Afro-Asian nations. They assured me there was *less* hate and *more* admiration for the West here than anywhere south or east of Cairo (skipping Israel, of course). Just as resentment toward the West is a fundamental of Egyptian politics, so is identification with the West. For example, Egyptians have had a total and almost uncritical love affair with American movies. More than once it was suggested to me that Nasser would be overthrown in a trice were he to ban U.S. films. As in Europe right after World War II, now in Egypt young people went to the movies to dream about life's possibilities, such as they were. They liked what they saw. Similarly, anti-Americanism in the press did not reflect or lead a mass feeling of animosity as it did in Indonesia or perhaps even more so in Brazil. Cairenes did not react to the news with quite the same passion one found elsewhere. The press was thought of as part of the government and, therefore, a thing apart. The revolution had, in fact, failed so far to create the nationalist zeal that might have inspired more immediate responses to propaganda events. Israel was the only sure-fire issue. Egyptians did not stew about socialism, communism, and democracy. Lacking a well-defined political identity of their own, they were less ready to fight over others'. Nasser's efforts at this level had produced only the vaguest political philosophy, which he regularly abandoned for any seemingly practical solution to Egypt's economic problems. His "Arab socialism" had little relationship to the tenets and concepts of classical Marxism. Even the students I met seemed less political than those in the streets of Djakarta. Few had ever met a Russian, let alone a Chinese. Soviet visitors were common in Cairo, mostly on cultural or diplomatic missions, but one never heard an Egyptian comment one way or another, pro or con, about any Russian. Egyptians sometimes shied away from Americans, I was told, as in the aftermath of the library-burning. But the moment would pass and the multitude of friendly contacts with Americans would start up again. There was almost no feeling of rivalry at any level, including the cultural. Many even resented and resisted the regime's efforts to promote Arab culture. There was no drive to compare cultures the way the French do. Instead, people were proud of Egypt's status relative to other nations in the Third World and were hurt that the United States did not recognize it. To account for our failure, they were willing to believe that it was all part of a Zionist plot—including the assassination of President Kennedy, whom most Egyptians revered.

My perspective on anti-Americanism in Egypt was partly shaped by an Egyptian woman, Mrs. Y., whom I had met at a dinner party on the evening of the day I arrived. She was the widow of an officer killed during the Suez-Sinai battle, and she had a ten-year-old daughter. Despite the ongoing emancipation of women since the revolution, no Egyptian was likely to ask her to marry him. Widows customarily lived out their lives in a kind of semi-retreat or, as Mrs. Y. called it, "premature burial." Mrs. Y. came from a professional family, had studied in Paris and Chicago and now taught reading in an elementary school. She was not typical, but her pro-U.S. attitudes seemed significant to me. In any case, she was 31, tall, and marvelous to look at.

I called Mrs. Y. a few days after the dinner party and she joined me for lunch at the only French cafe in town in a side street not far from my hotel. I had just come from my morning visit to the burned-out library. She wore a prim, dark suit and, like at least half the people inside the restaurant, dark glasses. She removed the glasses to study the menu. Her eyes were sloe green. Then she replaced the glasses and laughed. "We are coming out of the dark ages here," she said, "and the light is very bright." We ordered *cassoulet* and an Egyptian wine, which turned out to be very sweet. Mrs. Y. explained that it had been very difficult to get French wines since Suez. But in the past year, the French had made a comeback. The Comédie Française had played Cairo and French language studies were increasingly popular in the universities. "Language," Mrs. Y. said, "is very important. It is the forerunner of an attitude. The fact that so many of us speak French and English is something you should not forget." Then Mrs. Y. reminisced about Chicago. She had not been there for nine years, but she remembered "every minute of it." Her ambition was to return to the University of Chicago for her doctorate. "If I were a man," she said, "I should have been there already. You know, saddest of all in Egypt are the women. We have a joke about it: The only time an Egyptian lets his wife go ahead of him is when they are walking through a mine field! We are very repressed. A decent woman does not go out on a date after college graduation. She never dates a suitor and is only seen in public, at dinner or a night club, with her brothers or a cousin. Egyptian men do not court us. Instead, they watch us from a distance, check on our status, and ask our father if they can marry us. Otherwise, you must wait at home. On the street, you will not see a boy and girl being demonstrative, as in Paris. Each girl is under surveillance, even from passers-by, unless she is declassed or a foreigner. Egyptian men can be free as they like with such women. There is a feminist movement, but no important critics to denounce such repressions. . . . Yes, it is worst for people who have been exposed to the status of women in America. Returning home, you are very unhappy and you tend to marry the first man who asks."

When the food came, Mrs. Y. brightened. I asked her if she might later regret being seen in public with an American. She shrugged. "I am fatalistic," she said. "But right now, America is very much liked despite all the political talk. We know that you will give us the food we need. You are that way. If it were not that Israel was your fifty-first state, there would be no trouble. Our younger generation hates Israel. It is taught in the schools. Israel is the enemy. So, when you criticize President Nasser for his treatment of the Israeli question, we are unhappy with you. Everyone loves President Nasser and supports the Revolution. . . . Yes, the memory of Mr. Dulles is very bad. But President Kennedy—our schools were closed one week to honor his memory. When the library burned, your people protested the burning of the 'library.' They should have protested the burning of the 'John F. Kennedy Memorial Library.' Then all of us would have cried. . . . Why was he shot? We do not understand your violence. . . . Everyone wants to visit America! We are not afraid of the gangsters. People used to study in Germany and loved Germans because they opposed the British. But now we want to go to the United States because your education is most respected. . . . America made only one mistake. It is the mistake you have made all over the world. You accepted your inheritance of problems left over by the imperialistic British, French, and Dutch. There was bound to be a transition and you are unhappily in the middle of it. For the moment, you seem to be losing and that makes the communists in our world bolder. They are organized and they are pushing President Nasser. I am so glad you have decided to make a stand in Vietnam. I want you to bomb those communists. It will be a lesson not lost on the communists here!"

After lunch, we took a cab to the Citadel, a great Douglas Fairbanks fortress with exquisite mosques in Old Cairo. Then we ambled through the Khan Khalil Bazaar, up crooked lanes past clumps of shops selling jewelry, then spices, then hardware, then leather goods. There was a sidewalk shoe repair man cutting new soles from an old rubber tire. Mrs. Y. pointed out Armenians, Greeks, and Jews, the remnants of large ethnic communities broken up by the revolution's crude "Egyptianization" program. Mrs. Y. said she understood, but did not understand "Egyptianization." Mohammedanism was a religion of brotherhood that gladly accepted the prophets of the Jews and Christians. Nationalism was another religion, and the two had collided at the expense of Egypt's minorities. "Some of our most skilled people have returned to their homelands after generations in Cairo," Mrs. Y. said. "I think we miss them."

We walked on through a crowded slum. In the streets, women were cooking and men sat on their haunches, shaving. A magician had set up his act on an orange crate. He had a small crowd, including half a dozen pesky children who had watched him perform hundreds of times. His gimmick was a magic wand, a black stick with a nob on top, that worked wonders and was then offered for sale. There was a box of wands at his feet. When he saw me, the magician clapped his hands. "You see," he cried with delight, "the tall American and his nice lady have come to Egypt! Now he will go away and tell his friends what a great society President Nasser is building." Everyone applauded us. I tried to buy a magic wand, but the magician insisted on presenting one as a gift. "Tell them how an old magician thanked you for America," he said.

About four P.M., a cab ride and another world away from Old Cairo, we stood by the rail to watch the horses run in the sixth race on the grass track at the Gezirah Sporting Club. A vast sports complex close to downtown Cairo, the Gezirah had once been the exclusive playground of the British who built it. Membership today was more or less open to anyone who could afford twenty-two dollars a year and find a sponsor. Though its elegance had faded, it still maintained a soccer field, Olympic swimming pool, tennis courts, a nine-hole golf course, and a race track, besides bars, restaurants, dormitories, and two playgrounds—one for children with Egyptian nannies, the other for children with continental nannies. At the track, the grandstand was divided so that the well-to-do members of the club did not have to sit with the sixty-dollar-a-month cab drivers and ten-dollar-a-month sweepers who were otherwise welcome. The paddock crowd was draped in light tweeds. Close to the rail in the open-air track cafe, there were two fine-looking bearded characters, each wearing a white burnoose, seated with two feathery blondes. "It has been a slow revolution," Mrs. Y. said.

We bet three dollars on a gray horse that finished next-to-last. "Anti-American," Mrs. Y. smiled.

Monday afternoon, I called the offices of the morning news-paper, *Al Ahram,* to make an appointment with the editor, Mohammed Hassanein Heikal. I had written Heikal from New York, but put off any attempt to see him until I caught up with Egypt. Everyone I talked to in the past week agreed with what I had heard about him back home: Heikal's daily (circulation: 200,000) was a semi-official organ of the government; Heikal's column (every Friday) regularly spoke for Nasser himself. On Saturday, Cairo's English-language *Gazette* translated Heikal's column as news. Mrs. Y. had said she always read Heikal and assumed that, in his complex, convoluted, and pompous style, he wrote for Nasser's eye. At the U.S. Embassy, our people studied Heikal's works and also kept in personal touch with him. They considered him to be a two-way conduit, from Nasser to us and vice versa. Over the years, they said, Heikal's own attitude to-ward the United States had seemed rather more friendly than Nasser's, but his writing had still been a fairly accurate barometer of Nasser's moods: If Nasser was "going East", Heikal would go with him. I was warned it would be beyond him to speak except in terms of the Nasserite line. Like Nasser, he had convinced himself that he was marching with history and that history was good. He expressed the nationalist view of reality that was, willy-nilly, dominant in Egypt. Therefore, I wanted to spend as much time with him as possible. His secretary told me "El Sayed Heikal" had received my letter and was wondering when I would call. By all means, I should come around at eight P.M.—

Heikal, it seemed, was eager to talk. And over the next ten days during seven long conversations, his eagerness never faltered.

That first evening, Heikal was on the phone as I entered his office on the first floor of the rambling *Al Ahram* building on Mazloom Street in downtown Cairo. Gold-striped drapes, a blue-leather sofa, and a glass-topped cocktail table furnished the compact room with a dandy air. There was a single rose in a vase on his desk and a bunch of roses neatly arranged in a bowl on the table. An abstract painting hung on one blue wall, a painting with an Egyptian motif hung on another. The taste was Western Expensive. Heikal waved and pushed a cigar cannister toward me across his desk. He smoked Upmann's from Havana. At last, he laughed excitedly and hung up the receiver. To me, his first words were, "That was President Nasser."

Heikal stood up to shake hands. He was a short, tan, polished man in his early forties with a big face, hooded eyes, slender nose, broad lips, and big straight teeth. He wore a blue suit with matching tie, nicely coordinated with the décor. Heikal, as one American had commented to me, was "a little *shnook* created by a great gathering of forces in 1952-4 and ever since he has had to ride with them." It was a harsh but curiously sympathetic judgment, and I thought it would do for a first impression. Heikal now lived in one of the most exclusive Cairo apartment houses with central heating and air-conditioning. He had real estate interests and various State privileges; a chauffeur drove his car for him. He was casual about his good fortune, but he had an opportunistic quality that was irrepressible. He was *too* eager.

"I am enthusiastic about your project," Heikal said. "You can explain to America that she is always on the losing side because she doesn't understand what's going on." Heikal tossed me a match for my Upmann. He smoked his daintily. I noticed streaks of gray in his wavy brown hair. Tipped back in his chair, he said he was very worried about the United States. Stanleyville had consumed all of our prestige capital in Africa. "But—" Heikal said, gaily, "the situation can change because you cannot ignore America. America's power is so great, you must continue to deal with it. Our whole problem here in Egypt is a paradox. We are quarreling with America in order to become friends. We do not think Belgium will ever be forgiven for what she did in the Congo. But America—we have to work to forgive her!" Heikal pressed a button. His secretary entered with tea. Behind her came two production men with a problem. Heikal poured while solving the problem. He said he started work at ten A.M. and always stayed on until 9:30 P.M., after press-time. He was impressed by his own diligence. At last, the production men left, followed by the secretary. Heikal smoothly continued, saying how difficult it was to forgive the United States. "She makes endless mistakes," he said, "The situation in Africa is very serious; in the Middle East, very serious; in Asia, very serious. And in this situation, I am not impressed by Johnson's wheeling and dealing. At least J.F.K. and the Irish Mafia represented *our* generation. Johnson's Texas Mafia does not even have cultural pretensions. I have great fear of a man who gives an ox to the parents of every baby named Lyndon." Heikal said all this with his thumb pressed against his front teeth and the cigar suspended near his cheek. His flawless English diction gave off just the faintest echo of Arabic's soft round tones. America, he said, was going wrong everywhere in the Third World.

I said the Cuban confrontation had given Kennedy his first real opportunity to move both on domestic issues like civil rights and international issues like the nuclear test-ban treaty. Johnson had not yet had his victory. "Give him time," I said. "He might be very good."

Heikal smiled thinly. He said he had been to America seven times. He could not believe me when I spoke of Johnson. "He is *losing*," Heikal said, implying with a broader smile that his nation wanted to be on the winner's side. "It is not the communists who stand against the United States," he said, "but *history*. Winds of change are blowing, and America is in between. Evolution is irresistible. Communists identify with the will of the people for an end to exploitation. In Vietnam, America leaves no alternative for the people except communism. You are trying to freeze change. Look at it this way: In Thailand, the man you supported died leaving a legacy of millions of pounds. He was the importer of Coca-Cola and a creature of the C.I.A. In Iran, it was the C.I.A. that overthrew Mossadegh and supported the reactionary Shah. I know—I covered the story. Throughout the Middle East, the C.I.A. is the ally of feudal systems. You can read all this in books published in your own country. It is all in Wise and Ross, *The Invisible Government* [A book remarkable for its many errors of fact]. America everywhere resists change! But no power really can. History is irresistible." Hitler, I noted, had said the same thing. But Heikal was not offended. "Hitler went against history," Heikal replied. "America should learn from his fate. As far as we here are concerned, the essence of anti-Americanism is that the United States does not understand a whole generation in the Middle East. The trouble is that the United States is talking and behaving and entering into a dialogue with a generation that doesn't exist anymore. Everyone on whom the United States has depended in this area has either been assassinated or jumped before he was pushed down. The British thought Glubb Pasha in Jordan knew the Middle East, but he could not even predict his own downfall. Another generation was coming up. Even today it is very much underestimated.

"Listen," Heikal said, leaning forward, "I would like to give you the feeling, the ideas, even the complexes of this generation. Mr. Morgan. It is a generation that is here whether you like it or not. What is important is that we in this new generation have shared an experience together—this is what you are facing. . . ." It seemed to me that we were also facing all the old instincts, especially the lust for power. I had to admit Heikal was particularly articulate in justifying his.

In the morning close to eleven, I returned to *Al Ahram*. Heikal had been waiting for me in his secretary's office. Today he wore a light tweed jacket and an Oxford shirt in pale blue with a button-down collar. He hurried me outside to a waiting taxi. His wife, he explained, had claimed the family car and driver. Then we drove a short distance to Evacuation Avenue, so named because it was the road the British had taken in 1954 en route from their barracks to the railroad station on their imperial way out of Egypt forever. On the avenue, between a mosque and a Christian church and with a slum behind, there was a half-finished, fourteen-story skyscraper standing patiently as workmen scampered all over its surfaces. Heikal was very proud of this building. "Next time you are in Cairo," he said, "you will visit me here at the new home of *Al Ahram*. We are building it with almost six million dollars in profits earned in eight years since I took over. We shall have twelve presses, including color, plus airconditioning and space for expansion. The old building, where we are, the one that shakes when the presses are running, that is the old Egypt. It is a symbol of that complex structure, with additions laid on haphazardly, with no anticipation or allowances for growth, for the future. This new building is simple and still it is built for fifty years of expansion to 1,750,000 daily circulation. A nice thing, yes?" Heikal walked me up six flights, then down into the basement where the pressmen were already tinkering with new equipment, most of it imported from Eastern Europe. As we returned to the first floor, a gray, weatherbeaten workman recognized Heikal and seized his hand. "I want you to go up and up and up," the old man said.

After a while, we drove back to Mazloom Street. Heikal settled himself behind his desk and I sat nearby. He lit an Upmann with exaggerated pleasure. He was a man who had seen his chance and had taken it. And now he had decided to tell me how he happened to be ready. He said:

"My grandfather was a farmer in upper Egypt. Later he had a sailing boat on the Nile. Finally, near Cairo, he settled in a village where my father grew up. My father became a merchant, trading in wheat and cotton. Then he owned a mill. Gradually, his business focused on Cairo and he divided his time between the village and the city. He had two wives, one in each place. His first wife was an illiterate woman of the village. His second wife, my mother, was the daughter of a Cairo merchant. She went to primary school. From the first wife, my father had three boys and three girls who never went to school. He is alive today, age ninety-four, but all those half-brothers and half-sisters are dead. He was very strong, a typical Oriental tyrant. By the standards of the small bourgeoisie, he was rich, too. He owned three houses in Cairo, a house in the village, his mill, and his business. I think he was happy having two wives, both very jealous of him.

"Because of my mother, I went to school. I think my father was happy with me because I was wearing a suit. I was a small *effendi.* My half-brothers wore traditional clothes. My father would take me to visit the village, to the agony of my mother, and show off that I could speak English.

"In 1939, I finished secondary school. My father didn't want me to go to the university. He wanted me to become an accountant. But, like most of my generation, I was writing short stories and poems, and reading much. I had read most of the Arabic classics. I even read aloud for my father. He liked to listen to history, but not literature. We quarreled very much over whether I should get an education, especially in journalism and law. Also, he was a fanatical Wafdist and I was an anti-Wafdist. [The Wafd—a word meaning *delegation*—was formed before World War I and became the leading popular independence party in its day.] We quarreled so bitterly about politics that he would order me from the room.

"Anyway, I went to Cairo University and, at the same time, I had a job as a crime reporter for the *Gazette.* I did not write in English and I still don't, but I gathered the news and someone else wrote it up. I turned out to be a good reporter. At graduation, I switched to the Arabic-language press to do political reporting. This was the time of my life when I could have been a communist. I went to work for *Akasah,* a weekly news magazine, and advanced very rapidly. I was terrifically energetic, working 8:00 A.M. to midnight every day to produce enough so that there would be something left to publish after the British censors got through with us. I had many political quarrels and finally switched to nonpolitical reporting and foreign stories.

"Three years running, I won King Farouk's prize for journalists under age thirty. After winning the thousand dollars three times, I was asked not to enter the contest anymore. One time, I won it for a story on a cholera epidemic in the villages adjacent to the British camp at Suez. The politics of it were obvious because a British soldier brought the disease. It was a catastrophe of the British occupation, like the poverty of the people. About twenty thousand people had died when I went into the area. I lived at the center of the epidemic without shots. It was a very important event for me. I became very poetic and described the drama of death. Everyone in Cairo talked about it. They were astonished that somebody was reporting each day by telephone from this village. When I got back to Cairo, everyone knew me. . . ." Heikal said that he went on to Palestine to cover the 1946 Arab League Conference and the Arab-Jewish civil war. Then he covered the Greek civil war in 1947, the "Palestine" war in 1948, and the turmoil in Turkey and Syria. Before he was thirty, he was appointed editor of *Akasah.* Then the regime arrested him for an allegedly insulting article about King Farouk. He spent a day in jail, paid five hundred dollars bail, and became a popular hero. The revolution came before he stood trial. He married in 1955 and fathered two sons. After a brief stint as editor of *Al Akhbar,* he moved over to *Al Ahram* as editor-in-chief. Heikal had skimmed over the revolution, his role in it, and his friendship with Nasser all in one short sentence. I protested.

"Let me tell you about *Al Ahram* first," he said, "then we'll go back."

As I might have expected, he was not going to confirm or deny speculation about the use of Nasser's influence in opening up *Al Ahram*'s top job to a thirty-four-year-old who had spent most of his career writing politics for a weekly magazine. "The circulation of *Al Ahram* was sixty-eight thousand and declining," Heikal said. "It was a very old newspaper under competition from newer and more vigorous papers. All our equipment was new in the Twenties. The stock was owned by an old Lebanese family not interested in investing. So, I asked about my future. I insisted on a share of our nonexistent profits. I pressed for new machines and new facilities. I wanted not to be buried. So we got results. our circulation exceeds two hundred thousand daily. In 1964, our profit was one million dollars and, with that, we started the new building. We have been a cooperative enterprise ever since 1960. All two thousand people who work here belong to a congress of the firm and vote on the final budget. The Egyptian press, as you know, is not nationalized, but it can't be owned by private capital either. Fifty per cent of the profits must be distributed to members of the co-op and fifty per cent set aside for development. To get enough for the building fund, I had to convince the group not to take its share of the profits. Everyone wanted his share right away and in cash, so it was not easy to hold back for the future. But you have seen the result!"

Heikal arose. I stood up, too, thinking my time was up. Heikal indicated that he had something to say while standing and I should sit down. Then *he* sat down and we had a good laugh. He wanted to state his journalistic credo. "My readers spoil me," he said. "They pay too much attention to what I write. My job is much more. I manage the paper. I decide on major stories. Then I try to produce a responsible newspaper. We insist on respectability. We don't traffic in sensationalism. . . ." He seemed to see himself as a public puritan, a journalistic Nasser, one whom righteousness rewarded with privilege.

At dusk two days later, I again took my seat in Heikal's office. Heikal had just finished his column for Friday's paper. He offered me an Upmann, commenting that good cigars were now easier to get in Cairo since the Cubans stopped selling them in the United States. I remembered a special report from Cuba written by Hasidi Fouad, *Al Ahram*'s correspondent: "The Cuban believes that Cuba is more progressive than America," Fouad had said, approvingly, "that Spanish culture is more deep-rooted and distinguished than that of America, that the Cuban is sentimental, profound and cultured while Americans are naïve and shallow. Cubans hate Americans as people."

Fouad wanted this to be true and, apparently, so did Heikal. Wondering why, I wanted to understand the history of Egypt as he saw it and to imagine the conditions his generation inherited as they defined them. Heikal said one had to go back to the end of the eighteenth century. "All the land in Egypt," he said, "was owned by the Mamalukes. They were Asians, who had been brought in as warrior-slaves by the Moslem Caliphate. They took power, kept it under the Ottoman Empire and ran a brutal, shocking feudal system for six hundred years. They did not even provide minimum protection for the people. They simply stole taxes. There was no diffusion of culture, no spread of values that might have started a social revolution. The people of Egypt learned to expect nothing from their rulers and had nothing to gain from their battles, so they became very passive.

"Well, at the end of the eighteenth century, there were two big Mamalukes in Cairo ruling Egypt together, because neither could liquidate the other. Like most Mamalukes, they could not even speak Arabic. But, for a change, some of the sheiks and small merchants began to resist the Mamalukes. The ideas of the French Revolution reached them and there were demonstrations in Cairo. Then the Mamalukes agreed to set up a consultative body, to protect the mosques, and to repeal certain taxes.

"In 1798, Napoleon invaded Egypt. Americans could learn from him. He came with one hundred fifty professors from the Institute who made that glorious book, *Survey of Egypt*. Coming to fight the infidel Mamalukes, he tried to discredit them. He talked about freedom and made himself a Moslem. And he brought the first printing press Egypt had ever seen. There was a sheik of that time who kept a diary telling of the impact of Napoleon. Simple chemistry experiments demonstrated by a French professor amazed the Egyptians. It was the beginning of modern times for us.

"Meanwhile, Napoleon floundered. Nelson burned his fleet. Egyptians opposed importation of French prostitutes. And conditions in France took a turn for the worse. Finally, Napoleon left and the Ottomans tried to come back. One of the Turkish generals, Muhammad Ali, issued an edict that he and his family owned all the land in Egypt. Then he set out to be Caliph in

Istanbul. The British and the Turks made a pact against him, so he made a pact with the French. He tried to attack Turkey, but his fleet was burned. But more significantly, he sent eight hundred young Egyptians to France to study shipbuilding, astronomy, mathematics. When they came back, they were disappointed by Muhammad Ali's imperial failures and became centers of resistance to him. Then Muhammad Ali's son and successor, Said, grew up to be a playboy. He commissioned Giuseppe Verdi to write *Aida* for his opera house in Cairo. His most famous statement was 'Egypt is part of Europe.' This created an illusion because Egypt was still really behind the iron curtain of the Ottoman Empire.

"Then, in the 1860's, the civil war in the United States cut off cotton to England and roused British interest in Egypt. Because of the Suez Canal, the British became still more interested and, finally, they moved in during Colonel Ahmad Arabi's rebellion against Ismail, Ali's grandson, and Tewfik, his great-grandson. Arabi was badly prepared for the rebellion. He had made the great mistake of mixing religion and nationalism. He was always talking about Islam and could not separate out the idea of nationalism. It was the wrong way to make a revolution work. But he did take one important step. He asked the khedive for a constitution to define the authority of the people. He didn't get it, but that was a beginning. Then comes the twentieth century. . . ."

Since the rebellion had ended and the British Occupation had begun in 1882, it seemed Heikal was skipping eighteen years of important, late Victorian history in Egypt. The British record in that time was extraordinary if one accepted the premises of colonialism and the philosophy of the "white man's burden." British engineers, accountants, soldiers, and managers abolished slavery, increased the food supply, and reformed the army for a people who had had little military tradition. They suppressed industrial development and failed to develop a competent civil service. But they satisfied the most ardent nationalists of the day by marching on the Sudan to reassert *Egypt's* colonial privileges on its neighbor's soil. Heikal obviously knew all the details, but he had left them out to maintain the neatness of his historical viewpoint.

On Sunday morning, Heikal invited me to breakfast at the Gezirah Sporting Club, which I had first visited with Mrs. Y. I arrived early, but soon Heikal's chauffeur dropped him at the central clubhouse, then drove on to the playground with one of Heikal's sons and an Egyptian nanny. The morning was bright and cool and peaceful. Doves chirped and the rebounding sound of a tennis game echoed through the empty playing fields. Heikal wore his collar open with a dark green Ascot at his throat. He ordered our breakfast, which was slow in coming, and rearranged our lawn chairs so that we both might take the sun. "This sun used to be for Egyptian royalty and the British," Heikal said. "Now my son is in the playground." For a moment, he savored his triumph. Then he again took up his generational history of Egypt with no prompting from me. "Here was the primary situation," he said. "At the turn of the century we had five million acres of productive land. One-fifth of it was owned by the royal family, one-fifth by friends of the royal family, one-fifth by foreigners, one-fifth scattered, and only one-fifth by local landowners. That's the way it was in 1900 and that's the way it was in 1952. Fifty per cent of all our wealth was owned by less than one per cent of the people. This is what my generation saw very early. We wanted a coalition of all parties to face the palace and the British. We wanted to fight against foreign occupation and foreign immunities. And we also wanted to fight against those who compromised with the British and exploited their own people.

"Remember that the British had come in here to protect the interests of their own people who owned Suez Canal bonds. They ruled by terror until 1922. Then they mixed terror with compromise until the mid-Thirties. At this time, the Wafd was the main opposition, but my generation participated for the first time. Like young people all over the colonial world, we had one experience in common—now, listen, closely—in Asia and Africa and the Middle East, especially, we shared the experience of living in a so-called independent country ruled by an occupation force. We wanted full independence!"

Again Heikal seemed to feel justified in omitting a key fact. *Egyptian* imperialism in the Sudan was a significant factor in the

London-Cairo struggles of the mid-Thirties. But to mention it might have reflected upon historic Egyptian ambitions that Nasser himself shared with Muhammad Ali—as Stalin had shared certain ambitions with the Czars and, for that matter, as Lyndon Johnson shared with Theodore Roosevelt. Instead, Heikal stated his case as an injured party. The sun filtered through the trees and mottled his face, hands, and the empty dishes. *"There sits drear Egypt,"* I thought, remembering my Lowell, *"mid beleaguering sands, Half woman and half beast, The burnt out torch within her mouldering hands That once lit all the East."*

Heikal poured me a fresh cup of thick coffee. He recalled participating in his first anti-British demonstration while still a primary schoolboy. "I was twelve years old," Heikal said, "and I marched. The British fired on us and we gained prestige for the future." Heikal told me of his disillusionment with the so-called Glorious Treaty of 1936 which recognized most Egyptian demands except the key one—independence. Then the treaty itself was abrogated under the pressure of Britain's World War II concerns. Heikal passed the years of his later adolescence in an atmosphere of martial law and almost total corruption. "There had to be a final break between my generation and the older generation," he said. "I wrote a secret pamphlet saying the young should have nothing to do with the Wafd. Others expressed their separation other ways. Some joined the conservative Moslem Brotherhood. Some joined the communists. Others joined the Green Shirts, a fascist committee. Many young people were exploring the possibilities of all three groups. They had refused to join the established political parties because of the corruption. Both Nasser and I were asked at that time to join the communists. They failed to get us. Then the Green Shirts approached Nasser and the Moslem Brotherhood tried me. They also failed."

"You joined *nothing?*" I asked, incredulous.

"No," Heikal smiled, a disarming smile, "I joined a terrorist group. We were five boys with a car. We had big discussions whether we should kill British soldiers. We decided we shouldn't. So, in our car, we would pick out a drunken British soldier, hit him on the head with an iron bar, and speed off. We were never caught. . . . Soon after the war, there was a strong influence of Marxism in all of us and this drew our attention to the workers. A new labor class had been created by the war industries. So we sought to organize a committee around them, plus young people who had prestige because of the 1935 uprising. We held a Congress in Cairo and organized the National Committee for Students and Workers. It was not nationally prominent and it had some communist representation, but it was one of many vehicles for protest. The older generation was attempting to negotiate with the British but we wanted none of it. The British had set up a façade of parliamentary democracy and the Egyptians who benefited wanted somehow to preserve that façade. Our Committee led demonstrations against negotiations and helped bring down the government. There was chaos after that. Conditions in Cairo became extremely difficult. Everywhere in 1946, there were bombings. We young people were disillusioned by the four freedoms of Roosevelt. We had looked for American help because of the Atlantic Charter. But still, the regard for Americans was high because you had won the war and because we had not lost all our illusions about Roosevelt's promises. We favored Roosevelt more than Gandhi, who was too passive for our violent needs. We nationalists were simply against the British and for independence and clean government. We quarreled with the communists over nationalism versus internationalism. We quarreled with the Moslem Brotherhood because they were reactionary. But we were all very passionate and very violent young men. A nationalist boy, an affiliate of our Committee, assassinated the prime minister. A member of the Moslem Brotherhood assassinated the next prime minister. A small group of young terrorists killed the Cairo chief of police. We had no heroes, only enemies."

"What about Nasser?"

"Nasser had become interested in politics about 1942 when he was just twenty-four. He formed the original organization of Free Officers in 1944. Most of this time, he was in the Sudan. In 1947 came the big change. Every important group was trying to agitate and infiltrate the Army to which the British had left the problem of security. In turn, the police kept the Army under complete surveillance. Nasser finally dissolved the Free Officers because there were too many groups in conflict. . . . Now, about this time, I was working for a pro-palace paper while writing pamphlets and organizing meetings. I was a 'words man.' And then came the Palestine War. In 1946, I covered our volunteers fighting the Hagannah. In 1947, I wrote a series from Palestine entitled, "Fire on the Sacred Land," that mobilized many people. In 1948, I went back to Palestine. So many enthusiastic young men volunteered! Nationalists, Moslem Brothers—Palestine was the meeting ground for so many elements, so many angry young men! We felt we had been betrayed. The Army had been given false ammunition. Guns were backfiring. All our armies going to Sinai and Palestine had to cross Suez and go through British check points. Even after the 1952 revolution, there was one night in Suez before the British evacuation that I shall never forget. I was already a well-known journalist and yet British soldiers stopped me on the Suez corniche and searched me for weapons. I had tears in my eyes! Anyway, the Palestine War was raging and we were losing while Farouk was going to nightclubs. I wrote a pamphlet in 1948 trying to analyze why we were not successful in Palestine. I said that the Egyptian soldier was being asked to defend a land he did not possess, with an army—the British army—at his back, led by leaders who feared the Egyptian masses more than they feared the enemy, against an enemy, the Israeli, who *was* fighting for a piece of land.

"So, new ideas about Egypt and especially about land distribution emerged out of Palestine. And a new coalition developed—army officers, intellectuals who had volunteered to fight in Palestine, and writers—"

Heikal's chauffeur with his son and the nanny had just then returned. Heikal nodded to them, told me he could talk five more minutes, and then went on about the "new" coalition [army officers, intellectuals, and writers], which was the same coalition that had overthrown most tyrannies known to history including the

one set up by the previous coalition. He said the new coalition
refused to join the Moslem Brotherhood or the communists. "Our
nationalism," Heikal said, "was so strong we could not compromise it. We had been so humiliated by the British that our primary goal became national dignity. It is still more important than
anything else. President Nasser was not angry when he told the
British at Suez, 'Chalk on your fury,' or when he told you to go
jump in the lake. Rather, he was emphasizing the importance of
dignity in himself and in the people. It is more important than
food."

"Truly?"

"You Americans!" Heikal said, crossly. "You continually under-
estimate the passions here. It is because you have had no revolution of your own for one hundred and eighty-five years."

On the next Monday at precisely nine-fifteen A.M., Heikal
began talking again, this time with his feet on the desk and an
extra-long cigar between his manicured fingers. He wore a gray
suit, brown Oxford shirt, figured tie, and alligator shoes. He
seemed to be enjoying our sessions and appeared to approach
them as a professor tutoring a valued student. Heikal wanted me
to know as much as he could tell about his youth and the culture
that shaped his attitudes. He talked about memorable books he
had read. None of the first ten he mentioned were novels. "At the
beginning of the war," Heikal said, "I was reading current
events. I wanted to read most André Maurois and others on the
subject of why France fell. I searched for books allied to my
political interest and finding out some things were not yet written
thoroughly annoyed me. I felt no book gave a clear picture of
Egypt and the British Occupation. One of my great interests was
American history through the Civil War. I was also interested in
the Spanish Civil War. I think I consumed a great amount of
communist material. Marxism was for me, for a time, the key to
all the answers. Later, I quit this mood. It is a mood that you
quit. But it is also a fascination. I was a poet when I was young,
age thirteen, fourteen, and then I quit. Nietzsche fascinated me
for a time, but then he failed me. Then I tried to establish a

relation between Darwin, Freud, and Marx. My thesis was that the three of them together had all the answers. One spoke of the evolution of the body, one spoke of inside the body, and one of the needs of the body. . . . I was also interested in classical music and trying to convince friends to listen."

Heikal began pacing. "I met Nasser first in 1948," he said, "against this background: I had written a series saying that it was dangerous to diminish the Hagannah by calling it a 'Zionist gang,' and the prime minister of Egypt said I exaggerated the danger. But when our armies reached Palestine, he allowed no newspapermen to cover the war. There would only be press releases. [Nasser did the same during the Yemen campaign.] But I had contacts. I went by plane to Amman, by car to Jerusalem, and on foot to join the Egyptian army about eighteen kilometers away. When I reached the place, the army was gone. I moved on, was fired at, and finally found our army. Then I walked back to Jerusalem and flew to Cairo with my story. The military censor said I couldn't publish unless the Minister of War approved. His reputation was very hard. But he was likeable and, I think, he was courageous. I told him my story and I asked him, 'What shall I tell the people?'

"He let me publish and then I returned to Palestine. I was the only Egyptian correspondent there. The whole war was my private estate. So, sooner or later, I had to meet Nasser. He was a major then, commanding a post in a Palestine settlement. We met briefly. Some of his friends had been producing a handwritten newspaper, but much about the Free Officers was still very secret. Nasser was very cautious. . . . We met again in Cairo after the armistice, only briefly, and then we did not meet for a long time.

"Those were strange times. In 1949, our forces had a hard year in Palestine. Everyone felt betrayed. The Jordanians met secretly with Mrs. Golda Meir. Farouk became increasingly repressive. The Wafd came to power with a policy of surrender. Inevitably, by 1951, guerrilla resistance started. It was made up of men who had fought in Palestine, plus students, workers, and writers, without any real leadership. But an incident was bound to occur and one did. Some of our police in the Suez Canal area refused to obey British orders and the British surrounded their post. Then, while business-as-usual went on in Cairo, the Palace ordered those men to fight to the last. And the British killed every one of them. After that, nothing could stop the revolution. Early in 1952, rioters set fire to Cairo—I wrote that the fire was a political revenge against royalty's indifference to the problems of the people, and social revenge for the food we didn't have. The Wafd government was kicked out and Farouk tried to run things himself. Then I wrote a satire on Farouk and was arrested. But the underground was now going strong. I met Nasser for the third time. There was a long discussion between us and after that, he recruited me. Finally, July 23, 1952, came the revolution. We were free!"

With that, Heikal seemed to struggle with a rush of emotions. His eyes opened wide and full, brimming with tears. But he also smiled and shook his head. After thirteen years, what did all this mean? Heikal was not one to cry over an old victory or smile at ironies. Rather, I thought he had the gifted raconteur's ability to play all the roles and to believe in each for so long as the audience remained at his feet. My wife's father was like that. He would laugh and cry telling you a story, not for himself, but to make you feel what should be felt. He always moved me and, this time, so did Heikal. I could imagine them then crying for joy while wondering what to do next. But I could not imagine Heikal himself feeling this way in February, 1965. Too much had happened in between.

That evening in the same place, Heikal continued. I had asked him to tell me what the revolution was *for*, besides getting rid of the king and the British. "The point is that a new generation had come to power," he said. "Beyond that, it was very difficult. No one knew what to do. We could say what we didn't want, but we—Nasser, especially—wanted to say what we did want. After the Cairo fire, there had been revolts all up and down the Nile. But we had power and no plan. All the revolutionaries were amateurs. The established political parties were identified with the old society. Ideas floated in the air, but none concrete. We argued about everything, including what to do about Farouk. The majority of us wanted to execute him. We discussed assassinations. But Nasser wanted no assassinations. There never was a less bloody revolution. We tried to get the Wafd to rule, but they refused the land reform. The first government therefore included everybody except the communists and the Moslem Brotherhood. All through 1953, no one knew what to do. There were so many, many discussions—no dogma, no politics, just ideas—until we came to two main points. One was that the revolution's leaders should become politicians to avoid the experience of Latin America with military dictatorships. The second point was to achieve reforms quickly through bypassing the traditional bureaucracy. We confiscated all the money of the royal family—over sixty million pounds—and put it into social service projects. We sent missions everywhere to get ideas. And Nehru came here: One day, when Nasser and I were on a trip down the Nile, we asked Nehru to tell us about planning—"

I interrupted to describe an interview Nehru had given me during the Sino-Indian "border war" in 1962. Heikal said he loved Nehru and still loved India without Nehru. "You know," he said, "Mr. Eisenhower was correct about the domino theory in Asia. One reason, perhaps the *main* reason, I do not like American foreign policy is the danger it makes for India. We may lose India."

I was not certain I had heard him right. He seemed to be using "we" in the sense of we two, the United States and Egypt, or in the sense of all of us, Egypt, the United States, and other nations comprising the West against Them, the communists in the East.

"We may lose India," he continued, "because the United States does not clearly see its role in the world. The United States misses the point that freedom requires an environment. Instead, she thinks about balancing things off so that she can concern herself with the Great Society. It is a wrong idea. You will tend that way to isolate America and, as the Marxists say, intensify the contradictions. The rich will be getting richer and the poor relatively poorer. Soon, the poor countries will begin to fall and we will lose India."

Heikal nodded his head to emphasize his feeling of sincerity. It was as though he wanted me to believe this no matter what I might think of his interpretation of history so far. I denied that we had been missing his point. It was part of America's messianic impulse to want an environment for freedom. Even Dean Acheson, I recalled, had used that phrase or something close to it. But in trying to create that environment for freedom in the workaday world we couldn't even keep the peace, let alone introduce a Golden Age. I said I thought we in the West, including myself, had little real faith in this impulse and, each in his own way, lived in anticipation of The End.

Heikal snorted impatiently. "American pressure and our reaction to it," he said, argumentatively, "shaped this generation in Egypt. In 1953, the problems presented to us by Mr. Dulles helped us decide what we wanted. Talking about defense of the Middle East, Nasser was saying to Dulles he did not like the proposal of the United States that the British remain in Egypt. Nasser said, first of all, Egypt must be free, then we can decide on defenses. He said it would be queer to make agreement to a military pact against the Russians whom we had never seen while the British, who had been here seventy years as aggressors, remained. So, this is how we developed nonalignment. It is a policy matured through the reaction against your pressure for a military pact. We said, first, we want to be free. To that end, we would resist all aggressors. And right then, the British were aggressors. Probably someday, the Russians would be aggressors. But anyway, we wanted to be free to make our own decisions. Well, the British left in 1954. But then there were pressures against us from the Israelis. They raided us and we needed arms. In 1955, Mr. Dulles promised us arms, but we did not get them. So we went to the Russians and bought arms. Meanwhile, we had the problem of economic development. Out of this problem came the idea for the High Dam at Aswan. The Americans and the British had offered to build the Dam to balance against the Russian arms deal. But your mood changed. You were really cross with Egypt, So then, the High Dam crisis created the Suez Canal crisis. During that period, we decided to Egyptianize—not nationalize —all the British-owned banks and insurance companies. We wanted Egyptians to buy the banks. But then, we didn't want to create more concentrated wealth. So we put the banks under government control. During the Suez battle, we learned that an attack on the British here would cause them to bomb and destroy what they had. This created a belief that the real owners of a country are those who will defend it. The capitalists wouldn't. However, in 1957, the United States blocked millions of dollars and the British froze our sterling so that Mr. Dulles could carry out the British Middle East policy by other means. We needed to buy wheat and medicine, but you wouldn't release our funds. So, you forced us to become self-reliant, to industrialize and we went again to Moscow, this time to get the money for development. . . . We have stood up against the West and have been subjected to a horrible campaign of distortions. If you are outside, you hear we have concentration camps. But the fact is that *never* did we arrest more than four hundred people for political activity and today none are in jail. All the communists are free. All the Moslem Brothers, too. All emergency laws have been abolished. The amount of freedom of the press enjoyed by *Al Ahram* is not enjoyed by the New York *Times*. There is fear here among one class, the millionaires, who lost something. They don't speak because they don't feel secure. But what they would have to say makes them afraid of the *people!* We have found that socialism is necessary. It is the only way for an underdeveloped country. But we don't believe in a dictatorship of the proletariat. We don't believe in wiping out private property. We believe in restricting private property. I think we are giving a new experience to the underdeveloped world."

I felt my time might be running out. And I saw no point in arguing with Heikal about his absurdities—freedom of the press in Egypt, indeed! So, I asked him one last question: "What could change your feelings about us?"

"It is mostly up to the United States," Heikal said. "You must admit you are the stronger partner. Developing nations sometimes speak loudly just to prove they can speak their minds. So, first of all, you must be the more rational.

"Second, you must realize the interests of the United States are not always the interests of Egypt. There are things important to you that are not as important to us. Even communism. You have a standard-of-living. The Egyptian peasant has none. You have something to lose, he has nothing.

"Third, there is no fixed pattern for development of a new nation. Our way is our way.

"Fourth, you must have knowledge of Egypt. It is more basic than knowledge of communism. You cannot teach us how to fight communism in Egypt. It is an Egyptian question. No free people is prepared to accept tutorship.

"Fifth, even if you do care about us, even if the interests of General Motors are ours, you cannot deprive a man of the experience of trial and error, even if what you have to tell him is right.

"Sixth, you must be courageous enough to admit that people in other countries can think for themselves. What is this crazy, curious involvement of yours with the imperialist powers? And your involvement with others through the intervention and meddling of the C.I.A.? Because of the nuclear stalemate, communism will conquer internally, if at all. You should understand, therefore, that the national front against communism cannot be maintained by agents and conspirators, but only by nationalists.

"Finally, there is the overall problem of your attitude. The American attitude must be examined. Americans tend to confirm the picture of the ugly American. I am sorry to say that, because I know the picture is wrong. But now, today, you must ask yourself why is it a blessing for a man whom you make an enemy and a curse for one you make a friend? You proclaimed Nasser your enemy and insured his popularity. Why is it that all the men whom you befriended here in the Middle East are either dead or out of office? The king of Sudan was dethroned. Shavron of Lebanon was kicked out. Meneres of Turkey, kicked out. King

Abdullash Ibn Al Hussein of Jordan, assassinated. King Faisal of Iraq, assassinated. Prince Olas of Iraq, assassinated. Why is it that you are associated with only the most reactionary forces and against history—against life? Can you tell me who is popular in his own country and is also a friend of the United States? In Africa, all are against you—Nkrumah, Gbenye, Sekou Touré, Ben Bella. Who are your friends? You have only Tshombe, Haile Sellassie, and the Nigerians. You're losing people like Nyerere in Tanzania, people who started as your friends. All the strong leaders are unfortunately against you. Their relations with the Soviet Union are far better. Why? Ask yourself why. Can Tshombe be the champion of liberty in Africa?"

"Can Nkrumah?" I asked.

But Heikal went on. Groping for a perfect example of our folly, he came up with the good-will tour of Lyndon Johnson as vice-president of the United States. "His one stop in the Middle East," Heikal cried, "was in Lebanon! Johnson did not visit Nasser for fear of building him up. But he should have seen it the other way. If he had visited Nasser, it would have been a tax on Nasser and a profit for the United States. Given the mood of the Arab world, Nasser would have been the one to pay for the visit. . . . Once I was asked what I thought of Nasser visiting Kennedy in the United States. I believe there was something in Kennedy that Nasser liked. Their exchange of letters was very important. There was a mutual sympathy. But I felt that Washington would not be the place for them to meet. Nasser had only been in America once, for the United Nations. Deliberately, he restricted his movements between the airport, his house, and the General Assembly. Yet, all along his route, there were people booing him. I said I thought a Nasser visit would stress our differences, not our basis of friendship. He would find the American press lecturing him and hostile to him. He would not swallow this. He would express himself. So I advised against the visit. He can only go to America as a friend with a right to differ, but the pressures of groups in the United States make this impossible. A visit would have worsened relations rather than helped them. So, I suggested that Kennedy visit the key countries in the underdeveloped areas. Egypt, India, and so on. I would venture to say he would have had a heartier welcome in the so-called danger spots than in countries you consider your friends. Whether Johnson would get the same welcome, I can't say. We don't know Johnson yet."

By this time—it was the tag end for Heikal and myself—he had regained his good humor. Heikal said he hoped he had helped me and that, through me, he might have his say before the American people. He asked for my card so that he might call me on his next visit to New York. He even promised to ask Nasser for an interview for me. "You cannot understand the revolution unless you meet him in person," Heikal said. I told him I would gladly spend a few extra days in Cairo on the strength of his promise. Then we shook hands and I left. I walked in the sun through the welter of Mazloom Street. Furious newsboys hawked the late morning *Al Ahram* as though El Sayed Heikal's vigor were distributed along with his newspaper.

At lunchtime, I headed for a cafe I had found not far from the American University of Cairo (AUC). In Egypt, there were about five hundred foreign-supported schools with more than four hundred thousand students, but AUC was the only one above the secondary school level. In contrast to the European style of other Egyptian universities, AUC promoted our elective system for its one thousand students. But it was no different than the others when it came to government surveillance and control. The Nasser regime understood the power-potential of university students.

Passing the AUC gate and the impressive college building behind, I bumped into a student whom I had met earlier that week at a free lecture. He was a dark, rotund intellectual from M., a town in upper Egypt, and I shall call him Abdel. Abdel had told me he chose AUC to escape the "the deviousness of academic life" at the more competitive state-run universities. He also said he felt most comfortable with Westernized Egyptians and Europeans and Americans because they were "straightforward as people." Abdel knew that he was outside the mainstream of Egyptian politics. But he was convinced that anti-Westernism in Egypt was "all on the surface." He told me people "down deep" admired the West. "Anti-Westernism," he had said, "is all politics. Even Nasser's daughters are Americanized. Go to Cairo University. Sixty thousand students go to school free, almost all Westernized by the experience. Their favorite music is American and Italian rock 'n' roll. Their favorite song, you know it? It's 'I left my heart in San Fran-cisco'!"

Now Abdel seized my hand, happy to see me again. He insisted that I join him and his brother Ahmed at a nearby restaurant for a luncheon of chicken and *tamia,* which is an irresistible fried cake made of mashed beans, onions, and garlic. A happy little man wearing an undershirt and a long apron was cooking a batch on a wood stove as we entered an immaculate dining room with cotton-covered walls and a ceiling fan. Abdel spotted his brother at a corner table studying the menu chalked up on a portable blackboard. Abdel had told me Ahmed was once an ardent supporter of the revolution and, in the early days, contributed his technician's skills to one of Nasser's key programs. Then, in the early Sixties, Ahmed had opted out. Ahmed was fat like his brother, but fair-haired and at least fifteen years senior. He wore sunglasses and seemed to have only one voice level: *sotto voce.*

A waiter with clean fingernails brought *tamia,* chicken, a cheese dip, Arabic flat bread, and tea. For dessert, there was *baklava* or rather, an Egyptian version of it, so sweet my teeth ached at the sight of it. All this time, Abdel tried to get Ahmed to talk politics. Ahmed said he did not live in fear, but that he did not wish to live in fear tomorrow. I told him Heikal said only millionaires had been frightened by the revolution. Ahmed laughed, but he did not take the bait. We finished our coffee. Then, as we were about to leave, Ahmed changed his mind. "This is the real situation," he said. "Above all, the Israeli problem gives Nasser justification for restriction of travel, control of priorities, and other repressive measures. He does not have enough courage to let the people swing. I see at least ten years of hard times ahead. . . . No danger now, at this moment, of counterrevolution. Socialism was first a political device enabling us to take over banks and insurance companies during 1958, and limiting the possibility for counterrevolution. Now socialism is the state religion, along with Arabism and neutralism. Also, the State wants dignity, prestige, and honor. Which means we can behave badly towards others but not vice versa. We are an adolescent nation and this aspect is not attractive. . . .

"We can also become extremist when we taste victory, as in this dispute with West Germany over arms to Israel. Most of the time, Nasser and other intelligent Egyptians know that Israel can clobber any combination of Arab states in a fight. The Syrians are the only ones who might still want to test this. Yet, Egyptians get rambunctuous when things seem to be *slightly* going our way. If the United Nations' troops were removed from the Gaza strip, Egypt would have to be more cautious because, essentially, the U.N. is holding Israel back. We simply do not have manpower in quality equal to Israel regardless of weapons balance. . . .

"I am very depressed by the tragic cycle that seems to be moving here. It leads first to political repression, then economic depression, then military aggression. . . .

"But there is still a chance here, as everywhere, as long as there is peace. Where is Nasser going? East? Neutral? West? The answer is only in his mind. Two of his most accomplished aides have just resigned over his arbitrary decisions. We get no reports on Yemen, on lives lost or money spent. Only Nasser knows what is going on and Heikal publishes only what Nasser wants. Actually, we have no censors, just one hundred per cent government control of editors who censor themselves. People do not know what goes on inside Egypt. *You* don't know. I don't know where we are or where we're going. Under Farouk, at least, there was freedom. People were glad to overthrow him, but there was liberty. . . .

"Nasser's original intention was to give the people freedom. He wanted to let us talk. But he was not one who liked criticism and so he turned down his old principles. Gradually, he became a dictator, just what he said he would never become. He would not listen to old friends or diverse opinions. He probably does not know himself what is going on now. . . .

"I have no quarrel about socialism. It is right for Egypt. But Nasser wants to do it in one night. He has picked the wrong people to run it. They are all trying to industrialize too fast without realizing that the country is dependent on imports of raw materials. If the imports fail to come in, we collapse. Many experts warned against industrializing too fast. But your friend, Heikal, wrote that the experts should take orders from Nasser. Nasser did not want to hear the bad side of the story. But now, he's got so many troubles!

"Nasser has been in Yemen since 1962. There may be fifty thousand of our troops there today. Everything, even water, has to go there by ship. It costs one million dollars a day. Nasser thought it would last only a few weeks. The idea was to cover his failure to unite Egypt with Syria in the United Arab Republic. He wanted prestige, now he is losing money and men. He spends money for armaments instead of industry. This is hard currency— thus, in 1952, Egypt's reserves were six hundred million dollars. Now we are in debt one hundred and twenty million dollars. Incredible!

"Men like Nasser always develop an international crisis when the people are about ready to complain about domestic woes. The people like him, you know, and he likes them. He wants to do a good job, I think. But he has great ambitions. He does all right in international relations, but the *fellahin* still suffers, and our industry still lags behind. Imagine—Egypt's exports were more valuable *before* the revolution! Nasser has the geography books in school written to say that we are successful as a country because we have raw materials and markets. But, the fact is we don't have real markets. Sometimes we must sell export cotton at a loss in order to get hard currency. Nasser is surrounded by sycophants who won't tell him the truth. It is like Indonesia. Newspapers are inadequate. Ministers don't know what's going on. No one knows! But things are going badly—never before have people in Cairo stood in line for meat, chicken, even toilet paper. Nasser will look for crisis to cover his domestic trouble. . . .

"Nasser made a choice. He wants to bring Egypt into the twentieth century without passing through the nineteenth. This is a decision that does not examine its own premise. The question is whether a man has a right to sacrifice the lives of those now alive for a political dream of the future."

Suddenly, Ahmed took off his dark glasses. He was sweating under each eye. "My answer is no," he said.

"But what is the alternative?" I asked.

"Sir," Ahmed said, "if an American does not know the alternative to tyranny, then I have nothing more to say."

On Wednesday, February 24, Walter Ulbricht arrived in Cairo. Next morning, Heikal phoned to say the interview with Nasser could not be arranged. I believed that he had tried, so I thanked him and told him I would be leaving on Friday for Nairobi.

Thursday afternoon, I kept an appointment that Mrs. Y. had made for me with the seventy-year old playwright and novelist, Tewfik el-Hakim. Twentieth century Arabic literature claimed el-Hakim as its one indisputably great man. Early in his career, he wrote plays about classic Western themes. Later he shifted to Arabic and Islamic subjects and still later shifted again to revolution. He wrote plays to be read, yet the chief distinction of the Cairo theater stemmed from performances of his works. Egyptians appreciated his honesty and his taste for irony. Mrs. Y. told me he was probably the one man in Egypt who could speak his mind on any subject without fear. His office in the *Al Ahram* building suggested that he might be under Heikal's wing. But Mrs. Y. argued that el-Hakim's presence in Heikal's midst was one more of Heikal's privileges. In any case, I found el-Hakim in a good-sized but barren room overlooking Mazloom Street. He was a tiny man, very alert, with a white mustache and thinning white hair. He wore a blue beret. I told him my subject was hostility toward the United States to which he responded with a wave of his hand.

"The antagonism toward America is politics, not human," he

said. "American politics interprets every mass movement in Africa and Asia as communism and that is not true. The cause of these movements is not communism but the awakening of these people and their desire to live a good life. This creates certain conflicts with Western interests. The economics of it require certain adjustments. And all this, the Americans call communist and it is not true. That is the trouble with American politics. Yet, the American life itself suits many people in Asia and Africa because it is the life of liberty and fairness to individuals and to all classes of society. Egyptians admire American life very much, but generally, they feel politics is the problem. They feel they have so much in common with you that Nasser can be going to the devil, to the East, only as a last resort. . . . Anti-Americanism is only a reaction to American politics which is not going in the same direction as the aspirations of our people. It seems to you that communism is more appealing to the masses than democracy. But it is not communist theory that appeals, it is the communists who seem to be going in the same direction as the aspirations of the people. The farmer in the jungle does not know about communism. He only has a feeling. And America seems to him to be against this feeling and the communists seem to be for it. Now, the American politics can give this feeling for these people, if it only would. You know how! Show that farmer a Russian film and an American film. He will like the American film better because he likes the mood. Only the intellectual will like the Russian film better because intellectuals always confuse politics with people."

El-Hakim lit a long cigarette and winked at me. He knew he was good. He was an adorable old party!

"How did we get into this mess?" I asked.

El-Hakim blew smoke rings. Traffic noises floated up from Mazloom Street. El-Hakim closed his windows. Then he took up the theme of so many others. "America got into this mess," he said, "because her allies had colonial interests and rather than pursue independent politics, America chose to satisfy her allies, as when she supported British claims in Egypt and French claims in Algeria. Now, today, the essential thing is to show the problem clearly and allow time for the solution. The problem is justice. You know, it is impossible to comprehend the fact that a Martin Luther King does not have full rights in America. Likewise, it is impossible to comprehend that America does not take an attitude in favor of full rights for everyone. What is hated by us is the general attitude of American politics toward justice. The problem must be clearly stated now so that in twenty or thirty years we will see another America . . . If you can go to the moon, you can change your attitude toward justice. America must be loved, some day. It can't be hated all the time."

El-Hakim opened the nearest window and drew me to it. For a time, we stood looking down on Mazloom Street. Pushcarts and Cadillacs, creaking wagons and Volkswagen trucks crawled by. "The solution is very complicated," el-Hakim said. "But all these problems will disappear if you answer one question: how can we have a new economics? The basis of everything nowadays is standard-of-living. In Africa and Asia as well as Europe and America, the cinema and television give everyone consciousness of standard-of-living. Communism then gives people the feeling that they can ameliorate their standard of living. The communist answer is to give hope to poor people by attacking capitalist imperialism. This is the essence of the war between communism and the democracies. And the communists continue to consolidate their position while you are hated by the poor people. But, if you can invent an economics that will offer a good standard-of-living to all people without the use of traditional politics, there will be no war and no communism at all."

"That's a lot to expect," I said.

"From America?" he replied, incredulously.

6
Kenyans

At Cairo airport early on the morning of February 26, I routinely stocked up on newspapers and magazines for the 2200-mile flight to Nairobi.

The *Times,* a day late from London, was saying, "The developing countries' chances of solving their economic problems seem to be deteriorating fast as the richer countries grapple with their payments problems and interest rates rise. . . ."

Time reported "ritualistic anti-Americanism" in East Africa. "The three East African states of Kenya, Uganda, and Tanzania," *Time* said, "have one thing in common: they are all giving aid and comfort to the communist-inspired rebel armies of Christophe Gbenye in the neighboring Congo. Since the U.S. backs the legitimate Congo government of Moise Tshombe, who is a bête noir in the eyes of the black nationalists, East Africa was once again celebrating anti-American week." Kampala rioters had ripped up the American flag; in Nairobi, college students demonstrated in front of the U.S. Embassy; and in Dar es Salaam, President Julius Nyerere recalled his ambassador to the United States.

Finally, the *Egyptian Gazette* told more about a member of the Kenyan Parliament, an Indian named Pinto, who had been assassinated February 23 in Nairobi. His killer or killers, the paper said, remained at large.

I glanced through all this without much interest. I was poised for my first visit to sub-Sahara Africa, to the Hemingway country of my dreams. En route, at least, I wanted to forget about events and think about rhinos, elephants, and the snows of Kilimanjaro. So, I stuffed the literature into my briefcase and in a high, contemplative mood boarded a Kenya-bound British VC-10. Among eighty-five-or-so passengers were the foreign ministers of Ghana and Egypt and their aides going to Nairobi for a 35-nation conference of the Organization of African Unity (OAU). They sat up front in the first-class section. My own seat was in the rear on the aisle. My seat-mate was an Indian, a frail, dark young man whose skin was the color of tea-with-milk. He said he was on his way from Bombay, where he had been raising money to fight the Portuguese in Mozambique, to Nairobi, where his brother had just been murdered. He presented his card: R. da Gama Pinto. He said he had no idea who killed him. For the last day or two in Cairo, there had been speculation among journalists that the late M.P. had been taking money from the Chinese communists and was murdered for spending it indiscriminately. I asked Pinto if he knew why his brother had been shot, but he only grimaced and, shoving his hands into his armpits, embraced himself. Then I apologized for prying. Pinto seemed to like that. He fastened his seat belt, lay back, and talked very expertly about safari techniques. My anti-political mood returned and I was satisfied that one could fly four or five hours in a political vacuum.

Airborne and flying south and east of the Nile over gruesome red and yellow desert ranges, the plane was tilted about thirty degrees on its port wing affording a precipitous view of the scenery, even for passengers in aisle seats. We flew this way for some minutes even after the stewardess began taking drink orders. Mr. Pinto and I ordered martinis. And I said:

"Please tell the pilot we've all seen enough of the desert and—"

"That's the trouble," the stewardess whispered, her pale cheeks flushing red and her voice half swallowed in excitement, "the captain can't straighten her out. Something's up with the rudder."

"Mr. Morgan and I," Mr. Pinto said, "we'll each have two martinis."

In another few minutes, although there was no word yet from the captain, everyone knew the plane was disabled. Fasten seat belts. No smoking. There was a frightened buzz in the cabin, the sound of hoarse whispers tinged with regret. Why us? Why this plane? Why *now?* An African lady removed her head band and fanned her brow. An Englishmen with a C. Aubrey Smith mustache gnawed on an unlit pipe. And a heavy set man, probably a German, stood up, removed his jacket and glasses, and claimed a pillow from the overhead rack. He had read his safety instructions. But most of us stared out the port-side windows imagining the impact of our flimsy craft on those eternal, sandblasted rocks below. When our martinis arrived, Pinto and I drank them forthwith.

Momentarily, the port wing lifted and the plane seemed to fly on an even keel. But then, with an eye on the scenery, one could sense a slow turning. At first, I thought the captain had finally adjusted the rudder. But soon I knew that we were flying in a circle. And then the captain's voice spoke through the cabin intercom system.

"Our rudder is jammed," he said in an urgently relaxed official British voice. "Flying straight ahead, our wings dip over about one-third. If we correct for this, we fly in a circle."

Once more, the plane tilted to the port side. Presumably, we were flying due south again. The captain continued:

"Therefore, we are returning to Cairo after we jettison most of our fuel supply. Please remain calm in your seats."

The captain had not told us the worst of it which became apparent as he maneuvered to release the fuel in his wing tanks. At our angle of flight, the fuel inside the wing would flow past the jettison pipes, toward the fuselage on the starboard side and toward the wing tip on the port side. Thus, the captain would have to correct the tilt of the wings to get rid of the stuff. But this meant flying in a clockwise circle, which might cause us to fly into our own fumes—a danger somewhat increased by the tail position of the engines. For more than an hour, therefore, we flew in alternating postures—straight with wings tilted, followed briefly by horizontal and circling. We blew out fuel during the latter, then went into our list to escape the fumes. Pinto and I began to sing *Auld Lang Syne*. C. Aubrey Smith joined in. The African woman hummed. Soon, the tourist cabin filled with the music of strange voices. The stewardesses doubled the two-drink limit, but most people abstained. Pinto and I drank ours, however, and soon Pinto moved into the sloping aisle to comfort a fat and frightened Indian woman seated nearby and dressed in several layers of black lace. We sang "God Save the Queen" to the tune of "America," or vice versa, and "Bless'em All" half-a-dozen times each. These were the few songs that almost everyone seemed to remember. The English language!

At last, we changed course and flew back to Cairo. One final problem remained. Attempting to land the plane at a thirty-degree tilt would surely tear off the port-side wing before the wheels touched down. But landing on an even keel might mean circling off the runway. The captain had made his decision early. There was no practice approach. Flying on the bias, we slid into the pattern, dropped down to the runway, and seemed about to touch the port wing. Then the plane straightened and the tires screeched on concrete. But before the broken rudder forced the plane into a right-hand circle, the pilot cut the starboard- and gunned the port-jet. And between two long rows of fire engines and other emergency vehicles, the big plane rolled to a stop.

Later, during our nine-hour wait for repairs, I chanced upon my captain at tea. He was a tiny man with a salt-and-pepper brush mustache. He smoked a pipe with an Irish-curved stem. By all odds, he declared, that had been the hairiest experience he'd had as a commercial pilot.

"Really," he said, "it could have blown any minute while we were dropping our fuel. And the landing—best I ever made. . . . The trouble? Oh, somebody left a rag stuffed in the rudder assembly where it would do the most bloody good. But you can't say it was sabotage, now can you? It's why I don't like these V.I.P. flights. Anybody might've been after the foreign ministers of Egypt and Ghana."

I said my seat-mate had been R. da Gama Pinto, brother of the assassinated Kenyan M.P.

"Well, see—there you are! The bloody Chinese were out to get *him*. What's ninety-two lives to them?"

"For once," I joked, "it wasn't the C.I.A."

"How do you know?" the pilot asked, sucking his pipe, "How do you know?"

About eighteen hours late, another VC-10 with another pilot set us down on Nairobi's highland plateau. The sun was just coming up on a wondrously clear morning in what is, I learned, the best of seasons in Kenya. Though I stood less than one hundred miles south of the equator, the air was dry and cool—and faintly scented with hibiscus and bougainvillaea. My friend, Bill Attwood, the U.S. Ambassador with whom I had worked both at *Look* and on behalf of Adlai Stevenson, had sent a car to take me to my spartan digs, the United Kenya Club. It was a small, multi-racial residential club on the edge of the downtown district; room and board: three dollars a day. I had wanted to stay at the New Stanley on Kenyatta Avenue in the center of things, but all available rooms at the more centrally located hotels had been reserved for delegates to the OAU conference. Once I was settled in, though, I could not have cared less. Kenya was easier to love than any place I had ever been. Before breakfast, I hired a taxi to zoom south through town to Nairobi National Park. Here, less than five miles from the elegant "city centre" of modern office buildings and traffic jams, I saw a family of shyly powerful giraffes daintily chewing acacia shoots. A milling herd of Grant's gazelles minced through the high grass as though they might run for dear life at any moment. Further on, lounging in the shade of a scrubby bush, the king of the beasts waited for his breakfast. His wives, according to their proper function as lionesses, must have been stalking it. Life was real and earnest in Nairobi's park. The animals, as the tourist-brochure said, "are not fed artificially, nor are they protected from each other."

By nine that first morning, I sat down to my own breakfast

saddened by the knowledge that I could not compress the politics into a few days' work and spend the rest of my time game-watching. Two weeks later, when I left for Paris, I realized that I might have gotten away with it. The African leaders with whom I wanted to talk were not very eager to talk to me. To a man, they were angry at the Americans not only because of events in the Congo, but because these happened while President Jomo Kenyatta and our ambassador were negotiating to keep them from happening. After less than a year of independence, Kenyatta had been moving toward a foreign posture of realistic, anti-communist neutralism and was likely to be followed by most of Bantu Africa. But now he had to denounce American "intervention." Both Oginga Odinga, the Sukarnoite Vice President, and Tom Mboya, Minister of Justice, favored by Kenyan moderates and most Western "observers," followed Kenyatta's lead. Our African policy had attempted to satisfy both the colonial claims of our European allies and the anti-colonial principles of our own history and emergent Africans. Actually, it satisfied no one, least of all the latter. Amid great confusion, Kenyatta, Odinga, Mboya, and lesser players on the scene seemed to believe my project was more American racism. They were too polite to reject me out-of-hand. But they made themselves scarce and it was only after days of delay that I managed, one way or another, to get in touch with each. If I had planned a safari in advance, I would have had plenty of time to enjoy it.

Meanwhile, Kenya's population figures told much about the present situation. According to the 1962 census, there were 8.5 million Africans in more than forty peasant tribes, 180,000 Asians, 53,000 Europeans, and 35,000 Arabs: Kenya was over ninety-eight per cent African. Its largest tribe was the Kikuyu (1,700,000), second was the Luo (1,200,000)—and *tallest* were the beautiful Masai, who numbered only 154,000. The Asians in Kenya were mostly Indians: Hindus, Moslems, and Sikhs. Like the overseas Chinese in Indonesia, they dominated Kenya's mercantile life, especially in Mombasa on the coast and Nairobi. The Europeans were mostly British farmers, civil servants, and technicians.

To begin with the last: The Europeans had yet to adjust themselves to minority status; they had always been in the minority, but now they were compelled to *feel* it. While many had decided to pull out, most remained wrestling with the question whether to be or not to be Kenyan citizens. The demand for their skills still gave them enormous political power.

The Asians were less concerned about minority status, but more troubled about the prospect of losing their businesses during some future economic crisis. The Europeans, after all, could return to prosperous Europe. The Asians had only poor India to fall back on. Thus, they were more tenacious than the Europeans, but more cautious, too, and less likely to exert a positive influence on the African majority.

Finally, the Africans divided into two basic groups—the educated few and the illiterate multitudes. Outside of Nairobi (population: 267,000), Mombasa (180,000), and eight or ten smaller towns with a total population of well under one million, the great mass of Kenyans lived in the Stone Age. The average cash income per person for all of 1964 had been about fifty dollars. The British had worked some miracles during their brief span in Kenya. Between 1900 and 1963, they built Nairobi from scratch and developed an export trade worth nearly one hundred million dollars. However, they could bring themselves to build only about six thousand primary and intermediate schools, altogether incapable of educating more than fifteen per cent of the available children. One must assume they knew what they were doing. In Nairobi, as elsewhere in the world, apologists for imperialism liked to recount the benefits of colonization not for the colonialists, but for the colonized. But the British in Kenya had failed the test of responsibility. As, of course, we had failed, too, not only in the Philippines, but wherever the American Indian crossed our path.

The most striking difference between Nairobi and cities like Cairo, Djakarta, and Rio, was this city's tranquillity. Whatever passions might boil from time to time, there was an underlying quiescence that I found relaxing, and sad. I heard no pompous talk about "The Revolution." No one told me that struggle was an unqualified virtue. For the moment, at least, everyone seemed to have a stake in minimizing tensions.

Perhaps Kenya was a non-nation. Even the pressure of urbanization was missing—Nairobi reminded me of any one of several neat, clean, orderly company towns in the United States, like Flint, Michigan, or Worland, Wyoming. The streets were broad and straight and usually led you to ripe flowers, lush trees, and high, open country. Most of the Africans one saw were smartly dressed, even if the costume was a starched khaki uniform reminiscent of the old days. Every morning under my window overlooking Hospital Hill Road, boys and girls wearing straw hats and school colors strolled briskly to their classes. And beyond the downtown area, there were the lovely residential estates for the well-born, the well-to-do, and the well-placed of all the races. High hedges hid swimming pools, acres of trimmed lawn, vast flower beds, and roomy Fairfield County homes for members of parliament and African civil servants as well as the expected Europeans. One visited this Nairobi with pleasure, but always with a nagging sense of irony.

The poor were everywhere to be seen if one had eyes for them. And it was for them that the Mau Mau, thirteen years earlier, had been organized. Robert Ruark's reportage to the contrary, the Mau Mau killed no more than 1,750 people, about 1,700 of whom were *not* white. In return, the British colonial government and its white supporters killed 10,000 suspected blacks and detained 90,000 more in prison camps. Ruark apparently thought the Africans were barbarians because they believed in blood oaths and killed with sharp *pangas* rather than sten-guns. But now one asked whether the struggle had not ended in a mere exchange of bureaucrats, the new men as greedy for manor houses and swimming pools as their past masters. It was too soon to judge, but the essence of Nairobi at this time seemed to be that *nothing* had really changed. I loved Kenya, but I felt that the odds were heavily against her.

My first evening in Nairobi: Along with Bill Attwood and another old friend, Tedson Meyers, who was visiting Kenya on Peace Corps business, I was invited to dinner at the home of Phil Heller, our embassy's political affairs officer. About twenty guests, none African, assembled on the Hellers' patio under an umbrella of trees, drank a great deal, ate well, complained about servants, and discussed their own mood toward the current wave of African anti-American sentiment now focused in Nairobi because of the OAU conference. Since OAU aimed to create a sense of Pan-African identity among its members, appearing as a victim of the United States was a politically useful and distinguishing characteristic. Young men returning from study in the United States to important jobs, especially in government and communications, weren't helping very much, either. According to one of Heller's guests, an expert in such matters, increasing numbers came home far more anti-American than older men educated in America during the 1950's. By and large, he said, they were also substantially more hostile to the United States than young men of their own age educated in Great Britain or Kenya. "What are you doing to them in New York?" I was asked.

It was suggested that the Africans should make up their minds. "If these people don't want us here, we're liable to leave" was the sentiment of most of the Americans present. They were not joking. They were well-informed Americans speaking, and they were implying that Africa had less significance in the Cold War than anyone would dare say publicly. They were also suggesting that, in the absence of greater significance, our "responsibility" was less than compelling. For an African eavesdropper, one conclusion would have been obvious—if you wish aid and attention from the United States, invite the Cold War into your country.

Late next day, at the end of the row of government buildings on Harambee Avenue, I walked into a bright, new supermarket full of produce and merchandise at moderate prices. I made two tours of the place, first replenishing my supply of razor blades and then my toothpaste, before I realized that *every* customer was European, mostly fair-skinned women with red arms exposed in sleeveless print dresses. In the next twenty minutes, not a single African shopper entered. A color bar did not keep them out, but a cultural bar surely did. Did that same cultural bar also deny them certain claims on us?

Leaving the supermarket, I arrived at the cocktail hour on the edge of town where Thomas Quimby, director of Peace Corps operations in Kenya, lived in a modest bungalow. He had invited me to his reception for a new contingent of volunteers. Mrs. Quimby served spiked punch, soft drinks, and a dip made with Kraft cheese. I joined a circle of guests that included Quimby, an Indian school principal whose name I missed, and an African named Mwendwa who worked in the Ministry of Education. Without any prompting from me, the conversation revolved around African anti-Americanism, earned and unearned. The Indian, whose point of view may have been shaped by the new insecurity of his group, argued that most anti-Americanism in Kenya was communist-inspired or communist-organized. Mwendwa was more sophisticated. "Kenyans," he said, "have problems that are not solvable, especially the problem of unemployment. Twenty to thirty per cent unemployed in Nairobi. No natural wealth besides scenery and animals. A shortage of water, electric power, roads—you name it! This is very frustrating to the Kenyan. Therefore, he relishes the opportunity to let off steam, say, after Stanleyville. But I think you Americans tend to exaggerate these things. You are not doing badly here. And your competition is doing worse. . . . People are disillusioned with the Russians. The Russians give aid funds to Ghana in exchange for a good price on cocoa and then they compete with Kenya in the world cocoa market. . . . Believe me, in ten years people will see that there is a limit to what you can get from the East."

The Indian agreed, shaking his head from side to side. He said Kenya ought to "go West" if it had to choose. "The communists have a good argument," he said, "but it is antisocial in practice. The trouble with the communists is that there is a point of no return. You can't quit. That is what happened to the late M. P., Mr. Pinto. We believe Pinto was killed because he accepted money from the communists but had independent thoughts. His death taught a lesson to many Indians and Africans who have flirted with the communists. You can wind up as the odd man out."

"The mass of the people are not anti-American," Quimby said. "And the government wants to maintain friendship with the United States."

"But the pressure from the left," said the Indian, "it is very strong."

Mwendwa shrugged. He felt antagonism was to be expected and discounted. "Any country with a colonial background is bound to have riots and demonstrations. Our frustrations are innumerable."

"Are *we* then blameless?" I asked.

For a moment, I stopped the conversation.

"Well—ah," the Indian began, not wanting to offend his host, "perhaps the Peace Corps volunteers are too young. Some are immature and tactless. We admire their enthusiasm, but this is not enough. Older volunteers would be better. Before the Peace Corps, you know, other volunteer Americans came to us. There were young people from America who wanted to do manual labor. I suppose they thought they were showing the Africans that Americans are capable of it. But such a project was not sensible to us since Kenya has all the manual laborers it needs. And more!"

Mrs. Quimby interrupted with a bowl of potato chips and her American dip. Mwendwa grandly complimented her on the cuisine. I liked him. He was a trim, short, black man who ended every sentence with a quick smile. He said he believed the United States did not give other people sufficient credit: "We are not *so* dumb," he said. "We even have some understanding of communism. That is why you disappoint us when you—your C.I.A.!—use communist methods. These methods ignore political reality. The feelings of Africans are very real. We have had it up to here with outsiders telling us what to do. You must be more sensitive to that feeling. . . . Because, what is the worst that can happen?

We can go back to living the way we lived seventy years ago, before the white man came here. Thus, unless you are sensitive to our feelings, we do not want your money. We don't want the communists' *promises*, either. You must give the communists your freedom in exchange for promises of food and then, you don't get fed. Relax! We Africans need someone to blame for our frustrations. The witch doctor is always blamed when we cannot find the germ. America is our witch doctor now."

Later that evening after dinner with some of the people I had met at Quimby's, I was sitting in the bar at the Muthaiga Country Club, a fortress of unreconstructed British colonial nostalgia. Both the people and the place seemed to be echoes of past glory. The lounge décor was 1920-English Living Room in chintz and mahogany, all going to seed. And everyone around me, even the "youths," were advanced in years. The older gents wore mustaches over gap-toothed grins and the older ladies were faded, as though they had somehow missed the sun. There was even a broad-shouldered, gray-haired Scot wearing a black patch over his left eye and smoking a calabash. Shades of the Empire! All of them had eaten overcooked meat for dinner, and were talking about the decline of everything since independence. They openly despised their black waiters and, probably, the few new African club members inducted in recent months. "We did everything for these people and now look—ingratitude!" they said, each in his own way. Not one, however, could understand an American's pique at the ingratitude of, for example, British recipients of Marshall Plan aid.

Anyway, they were all sitting around hating themselves, Africans, and, I guessed, me, too, when yet another Englishman entered and, finding no other place to sit, took a chair at my table. He was a small, brisk man, dressed in a linen suit, who had lived in Kenya since 1938. We introduced ourselves, and he readily confessed to his own deep prejudice against Americans. "But it is more than that," he said. "It is also the weakness and indecision of American foreign policy that aggravates me. Look at the Africans—they are Western in language, dress, and education. Their money is Western and so are their transistor radios. They are simply waiting for the United States to create an opportunity for them to be pro-American. . . . What do I mean? Nothing can be done until you Americans have an idea of what you want and are willing to work to see that you get it."

The Englishman bought me a whisky. He smiled for the first time, apologizing for his vehemence. "Look, there is one positive element in sub-Sahara Africa—a genuine thirst for education and knowledge. If the great powers could manage a 'hands-off Africa' policy, if technological aid came through the United Nations, and if Africa was given peace to make a mess of its own—we would *all* be better off. The question is: what kind of a mess? You must study Africa with some idea of what makes for stability and growth and, I'm for it, *democracy*. Africa has political independence. It is now struggling for economic independence. But it has no spiritual independence. Instead of ideology, here they have phraseology. You have had frightful corruption here because you did not have the spiritual thing first. Africa's history since 1955 has been a wild inversion of Western experience. The middle class is based not on commerce and industry, but on a phony bourgeoisie of big government salaries, big cars, and big bribery. Sooner or later, the people will attack this and the Chinese are quite intelligently playing upon it. Over the long run, if they are the only ones not identified with corruption, they will win. . . .

"The United States of America needs some cruel honesty. To Afro-Asians, America is our natural heir. You are not English, but of the English. You play baseball instead of cricket, but it is all balls and bats, nevertheless. Like us, you are rich and white. Thus, *all* American protestations of sincerity produce nothing but anger, suspicion, and contempt. . . . I know many American liberals. You believe in 'involvement' and you hate 'indifference.' But you've got to be tougher and still not be disillusioned. You have literally thrown money at these new African states. The East Germans have thrown more money. And West Germans piled more money on top of that. Even a mature person could hardly keep his balance under these circumstances. And the African does not even know priorities. Here in Kenya you are seeing the best of a bad lot. The Kikuyus, at least, are hard-working people. They have been practicing self-help for fifteen years. Kenyatta and even Odinga have a grip on the problem. But here there is tragedy. And in a place like Gabon, there is chaos. It is no wonder Africa is a mess. You have had twenty years of cold war, the Arab-Israel struggle, the emergence of China—Africa is a battleground for all this."

Now it was my turn to buy the impressive Englishman a whisky. I told him I thought he had made out a good case for an unlikely event—American withdrawal from Africa. The Englishman clenched his fist and pounded the chintz-covered arm of his chair. He insisted that the event was not "unlikely". He said: "I feel the United States *should slowly withdraw:* Reduce your A.I.D. staff. Finish your current commitments. When you are approached for new assistance, don't refuse. Just shilly-shally in Congress, democratically. When your ambassador's term of office is over, replace him with a consul. No harsh words. Just slowly contract, withdraw. The fact is that the communists, and especially the Chinese, need America in Africa for an antithesis. But you will withdraw smiling. You will never show anger, for that is what the Africans want. They want you to lower yourself to their level of insult. That gives them the equality they crave. Better, then, to withdraw and let the communists make mistakes. The Chinese do not get along, really, with any other race. They will make mistakes and then the Africans will come to you."

"Why," I asked, "don't the English?"

"But, my good man, that's the point—*we did!* The original meaning of the word 'neocolonialism' referred to the decision of the British and the French to *pull out* of their colonies in the late Fifties. We did it knowing the people were not ready for independence. That way we avoided military operations and also actually lengthened the period of post-colonial *dependence.* If we had waited, more and more Africans would have been educated and would have become less and less dependent. The Americans and the communists stepped in to fill the gap and got burned!"

The Englishman knew he had shocked me. I laughed. No

American President, I said, has ever admitted a Machiavellian impulse. A withdrawal from Africa would have to be justified as a victory for freedom, democracy, and the sanctity of motherhood.

"Spare me from idealists," the Englishman replied. "They are always the first ones to use torture in wartime."

"That isn't fair," I said.

The Englishman retreated. "I only mean Americans have some-how adopted our ideals of the nineteenth century a hundred years too late," he said. "We put down the white man's burden and you pick it up, in the name of anticommunism. It's too late, sir. Africa is in for upheavals. The boundaries of these new states are colonial, not natural. In ten years, maybe less, the map of Africa will change drastically. You are fighting history if you fight for the status quo. Nothing that affects the vital security of Amer-ica will happen here for many years. Look at it realistically. You waited for the dust to settle in China, which has an ancient and viable culture. But in Africa you are not willing to wait—"

"We learned from China."

"No, you learned nothing from China."

After that cryptic remark, the Englishman waved his hand to show that whatever either of us said was of little moment. Then he relented for the last time. "It was W. C. Fields who had it right," he said. "He was on his deathbed, as the story goes, with his friends all around. And he was saying how he wished he had time to say goodbye to all the people he knew who had never had a chance in life. He spoke of the poor and the friendless and the exploited and the unfortunate. And his friends smiled—Fields had at last become a Christian. But then Fields lapsed into a coma and when he awoke again, his last words were: 'On the other hand, tell them to go f— themselves.'"

During my time in Kenya, I had long talks with three other Englishmen, all veteran colonials and all of whom reflected upon America's effort to pick up the pieces of British, French, Belgian, Dutch, and Portuguese colonialism in Africa. One was Kenneth Bolton, editor of the East African *Standard*, Nairobi's leading daily newspaper. Another was Henry Reuter, editor of a weekly news magazine called *The Reporter*. And the third was Malcolm MacDonald, British High Commissioner and former governor of Kenya. Bolton, a cold-warrior, condemned us for lack of subtlety. "You fought Tshombe in Katanga and supported him in Leopold-ville," he said. "You play the communists' game whether you are involved or withdrawn. Don't you realize Africans want to play no man's game but their own?" Reuter, a pragmatist, blamed us for indecision. "You have not decided what you want in Africa," he contended. "Do you want power or do you want to do good? Tshombe once said, 'There are only two things you can do to African politicians: bribe them or shoot them.' Africans hate Tshombe because he is contemptuous of them. But he knows this truth—Africans are not grateful people. When your goal is doing good, it means you seek gratitude. Gratitude! You will not even win the propaganda battle here with such a policy. . . . The danger is that frustration will force you to withdraw. This would be a fatal blow to pro-West politicians like Mboya, who wants to succeed Kenyatta. Better that you hang on for three or four years until the weight of students returning from the United States and Britain makes a preponderance in favor of the West." Finally, MacDonald, an optimist, wondered if we were sufficiently com-mitted to the long view. "The anti-American demonstration," he said, "may be a mass phenomenon studied better as a psychologi-cal event than as a political one. It is rather like the Beatles epidemic spread through mass media. Perhaps the Africans will get over it. And the Europeans, too. Everyone is still adjusting to the new order of things in Africa. Everyone is insecure. But I believe some day that feelings will swing back toward the United States. Have patience."

In short, the local British had varying opinions of American wisdom, but all took for granted our status as surrogate for erst-while colonial power in Africa.

During my second week in Kenya, I began to get some insight into the African point of view.

First, I met John Dumoga, a short, feisty reporter from Ghana who worked for *The Nation,* daily competition for the *Evening Standard.* The editor of *The Nation* was a Kikuyu named Hilary Ng'weno. Dumoga had invited me for a morning chat in his cubicle at the newspaper office to have his files close at hand. These, he thought, proved his point about the absolute malevolence of Dr. Kwame Nkrumah. Dumoga had fled Ghana "to escape Nkrumah's oppression" and to wait until the reclusive premier gave up "his dream of being first president of a United States of Africa." I asked Dumoga why so many African politicians who had been educated in the West, and particularly in the United States, chose to appeal to the masses with anti-Americanism. Dumoga hunched over his desk, smoking a Pall Mall. He said the whole problem was emotional. Personally, he liked what the Americans had been doing in Africa, supporting legal government at every turn even if it meant stirring up the mobs. It made sense to him to attack Tshombe when he had been a secessionist and to back him when he was the legal head of the Congo government. "Without legality," he said, "you have chaos."

Dumoga produced clippings from his writings to document his opinion. "If you ask anti-American Africans to draw up a bill of particulars against the United States," he said, "you won't get ten people who can actually point out what America has done wrong. And these ten would not be correct because they don't understand the concepts of legality. No Kenyan challenges the military aid Kenya receives from Great Britain. Yet, this is precisely the same kind of bilateral military aid that America furnished Tshombe in the Congo. Perhaps what you should do is let Africans buy military hardware from the Russians. Then, when they use it to kill each other, you won't be held responsible. . . . But you asked me why the politicians hate America. It is because America has power and uses that power to block them—I mean the leaders of Ghana, Algeria, United Arab Republic, Guinea, Mali, Tanzania, and Congo Brazzaville—from getting into the Congo. They want to take over the Congo physically and the United States is keeping them out. A lot of this goes back to 1960 when Nkrumah wanted to form a union of Ghana, Guinea, Mali, and the Congo. Everyone has forgotten that Lumumba was Nkrumah's protege. He even shipped a limousine to Leopoldville so that he could ride in it with Lumumba. Now, when his effort to make union failed, he changed his tune and did everything he could to prevent an orderly solution of the Congo problem. Just last autumn, he boycotted Kenyatta's *ad hoc* committee because he saw that it might succeed. So, you see, you have a very intricate situation with ambitious men willing to exploit any issue that moves the masses. . . . I would make two suggestions. One, if American aid is going to be continued in Africa, this aid should be limited to humanitarian services like education, transportation, and communications. America should get out of the military aid field. Secondly, America must be patient. There is no sense arguing with most Africans because they don't know what they are talking about. Rather, you should just explain over and over that even though you are white, you have no territorial ambitions and that you are helping people for idealistic reasons. . . ."

Dumoga closed his clipping book. He smiled. "You should speak to my boss, Hilary Ng'weno, editor of *The Nation*," he said. "He was educated at Harvard and is more anti-American than anyone I know."

That afternoon, I returned to *The Nation* to keep an appointment with Hilary Ng'weno. At lunch, I had mentioned his name to a Not-for-Attribution U.S. source, who volunteered a bitter evaluation of African exchange students. "The United States fills them with envy and jealousy," the American said. "At the same time, so much is done for them that they return with over-ripe expectations. Thus, the very goodness we show in the States eats us up here. The students return, greedy for success, and find that even good jobs don't pay much. They feel impotent, so they build up a sense of power in themselves by attacking the hand that helped them. Finally, in the States, they have learned that Americans don't have much interest in Africa. There is no U. S. population in Kenya and no U.S. economic interests. Yet, when Americans are insulted, they do not go away and this confirms their suspicion that they are up to no good. Thus, fear of our power and distrust of our intentions feeds on our generosity and produces Africans who really hate us. From now on, our student exchange program should be limited to the more mature graduate students and, instead of *importing* African undergrads, we should *send* teachers!"

After talking to Ng'weno, this analysis seemed imprecise. It ignored—at least in Ng'weno's case—positive sentiments that also seek expression. Ng'weno began objectively, attacked hard, softened, and finally spoke of the United States with affection.

It was about three P.M. when I sat down with Ng'weno across a long table in his air-conditioned office at *The Nation*. His paper, a tabloid, had been founded by an English editor named Charles Hayes backed by the Aga Khan. The Ismaeli sect, largest among Kenya's Arab-Asian minority, looked to the Aga Khan as leader. And, in turn, he controlled *The Nation's* policy regarding coverage of Ismaeli news. Late in 1964, the Khan submitted to pressure for Africanization of Kenya's press, removing Hayes and installing young Ng'weno as editor. Ng'weno, who had graduated with the class of '61 at Harvard, was a thin, broad-lipped, jumpy man, articulate but so intense that his words sometimes seemed to stick in his throat, then erupt in a clot. He often pointed a finger at me to reinforce a point. Yet, as I said, he relaxed toward the end of our hour together and seemed genuinely concerned about improving the present atmosphere. He said he had plenty of time to talk, having finished his column for the day. It was an attack on President Johnson's failure to continue the Kennedy style in personal diplomacy.

As had happened so many times before, the first question about anti-Americanism produced an extraordinarily long answer. Was it true, I asked, that American-educated Africans were more anti-American than other people? Elbows on the table, Ng'weno seemed to size me up for a moment. Then he said:

"The American-educated African today returns to his home to find imperialism and colonialism under attack. And the United States is associated with imperialism in this attack. So, the

American-educated African seeks to show his own people that he is not pro-American. That is why you find very few pro-American intellectuals in Africa. Intellectuals are the weakest group in every African country, so in the interest of survival they have to be more anti-American than anyone else.

"Moreover, discrimination in the States gives some Africans additional anti-American feelings. Ironically, British-educated Africans actually suffer greater race prejudice and yet they take greater pride in their British experience. I suppose it is because African students in the States don't stay long enough to understand the States, while the student in Britain has already had experience with the British as colonials. It is just that much easier to see the bad side of the United States. It is not an issue of facts with us, but an issue of feelings and emotions. Thus, the young, American-trained civil servant could not get a job in our foreign ministry unless he were anti-American. On a crucial issue, like the Congo, if a young man gave his superiors any suspicion that he was pro-American, he would be out.

"The politician, you see, wants the leeway to be pro- or anti-American as needed. Likewise, he wants to be independent of the Russians and the Chinese. You'll find no one in our Foreign Ministry who has been educated in the Soviet Union or China. The fact is that many Africans educated in Russia come home anti-communist. But the point is to be independent in order to deal with the situation.

"Today, England, France, and the rest of the old colonial countries are not big enough to matter. But America has been pushed, or moved by itself, into a position of seeming to defend capitalism all over the world. At the same time, America seems to want to control young independent nations. It doesn't matter whether or not this is true. What matters is that people have come to believe it. Crude anti-American propaganda is a factor, but the issue is too complex to be answered in this way. The masses of people respond for a great variety of reasons and politicians exploit this response in order to stay in office.

"The biggest count against you is your alliance with the former colonial powers. You are a friend of our enemy, so this makes anti-American propaganda that much more believable. Also, in recent years, on every issue affecting African emotions you have always been on the wrong side, culminating in the Congo.

"Look at the history of this thing. When the United States ten years ago was pushing the British, the French, and the Belgians to get out of the colonial business, Africans loved the United States. That's why so many of us went to America to study. But then you took a very inflexible position. You said you would support any legal government that asked for American help. And this got you involved in the Congo. You must somehow learn to face Africa with more realism than in the past."

Ng'weno sat back in his chair for the first time, seemingly satisfied with his discussion. But he lurched forward again when I said, off-handedly, maybe the United States ought to get out of Africa. It seemed to be the opening he had been waiting for: In the aftermath of events in the Congo—at that moment, white mercenaries were mopping up the hapless rebels—and with Tshombe scoring a surprise propaganda victory at the OAU conference, the subject of U.S. withdrawal was more than a topic for quiet discussion among Americans and their friends in Nairobi.

"African countries," he said, "must learn the hard way. Just recently, Tanzania sacrificed German aid—and now Tanzania will learn the cost of a moral stand. If they learn that moral values are more important than the money which is used to help people, then that will be a valuable lesson. Or, they may learn that there are limits. The point is that African nations today are in the dangerous position of taking aid for granted. So, it doesn't bother me when I hear that the United States, the Soviet Union, or any nation may be pulling out its aid, because going through this experience, Africans learn how expensive a move is and what it means. Both the French and the Russians pulled out of Guinea, and that may mean that Guinea is now more mature than the rest. It might even do the United States some good to pull out: While the African nations learn the value of American aid, the U.S.

might even learn that its dollars are not indispensable. The Africans would also have a chance to learn that if you want aid, you don't go around throwing rocks. On the other hand, if the United States is *not* going to withdraw, then the only policy that makes sense is one of selectivity. America cannot be friends with everyone. You will be most respected if you operate in your own self-interest. You should give to friendly nations, withhold aid from the rest. The name of the game is international politics, not religious morality."

"How, then, are the communists kept out?" I asked.

Ng'weno scowled. "That's not Africa's problem, but yours," he said, with an exasperated snort. "It is irritating that you seem to think you know what is best for us and that we don't know the difference between communism and democracy. It is also irritating to think that the only reason you are here is to keep the communists out. This is the great weakness of American policy. America doesn't give the impression that it is in Africa because it cares about Africans. When pushed, you always say you are here to keep the communists out. The easiest way to push the African toward communism is to tell him he needs to be protected from it. At least, you should recognize a fact of history. Africans tend to like people that colonialists and imperialists dislike. Russians are interesting to us simply because you hate them so much. People newly independent want to make judgments on their own and will tend to take a view opposite to the one held by their former masters. Is that not the lesson of *American* history? Africans are more intelligent than you think. Give them a chance to burn their fingers on the communists. If communists are that bad, they will find out."

Ng'weno slumped back in his chair. "What else?" he asked.

"What next?" I replied.

"Well, person-to-person diplomacy between President Johnson and African leaders would help," he said, echoing his column in *The Nation* for that day. "Our leaders do not feel Johnson has a personal interest. I myself would like to see better relations between Americans and Africans. If the worst happened, if the

United States pulled out, even that would give both sides a chance to learn more about their own values and what the value of each is to the other. Like America, Africa has to learn to face the world with more realism. Pretty soon, I hope, we will be over this hump of bad relations. Even now there is no way to avoid talking to each other, even if only to abuse each other. But let us hope Tshombe disappears so we can have some peace."

A while later, after I had left Ng'weno, I stopped on Kenyatta Avenue to ask directions of an African wearing a starched khaki uniform with black and gold epaulets. He was telling me what I wanted to know until, at the last moment, a husky white woman stepped between us. She smiled, condescendingly.

"Where do you wish to go?" she asked me.

"Well, this man—" I began.

"He's going to Duke Street," the African put in.

"Duke Street!" the lady said, and proceeded to repeat the precise directions I had just received from the African. Then she stalked off, no doubt whistling "God Save the Queen."

The African smiled at me.

"Maternalism," I said.

But he merely saluted and continued on his way.

There was a big, torch-lit, outdoor party Thursday night, March 4, at the home of Jaramogi Ajuma Oginga Odinga, for whom about five hundred diplomats, OAU delegates, civil servants, and friends turned up. Odinga was then Vice President of Kenya. Among the friends were ebullient businessmen, strangely silent women, and various drifters, including one barefoot man wearing pants, shirt, and the dangling remains of a Western-style suit-jacket—just the shoulder pads and the shreds of a sleeve and one pocket. Most of the guests had arrived and fattened before Odinga made his appearance. They moved into the large, well-tended yard behind Odinga's rambling, vaguely Tudor house. Here, attendants served beer and whisky at a makeshift bar while others spread out huge quantities of food on a long, scrubbed table. In less than an hour, people ate almost everything in sight and most of the liquor disappeared, too.

Then, when the proper glow had been achieved, Odinga stepped off his back porch and joined the throng. He was a Luo in his early fifties, medium height and overweight, wearing white robes and a white skull cap and carrying his flywhisk, a switch made of animal hair that symbolized the authority of a chief. He had a button nose, an expansive belly, and style—there was no doubt that he was our host. Odinga was the son of a poor woodworker in Central Nyanza not far from Lake Victoria. He had struggled for a degree in education at a college in Uganda and taught school for seven or eight years before going into the printing and construction businesses. Since 1948, he had followed Kenyatta, fought for his release from prison, and presumably aimed to succeed him. Among his drawbacks were his membership in the Luo tribe—that is, he was not a Kikuyu—and his leftist tone of voice. Odinga often admitted his willingness to spend money provided by the Soviet Union and communist China, but so far he had avoided the communist label. He called himself an African socialist and, in one speech, said: "In the cold war, we belong to neither camp. We belong to Africa." Hearing about him, I was reminded of Sukarno—but Kenya was not Indonesia. It was hard to imagine that Kenyatta's masses would one day follow Odinga.

Odinga shook hands with me and waved his flywhisk over our grip. He said he enjoyed visiting the United States in 1963 where he had gone to accept Kenya's UN seat. He liked central heating in cold New York, he said, but he did not like the weather in Atlanta. That, I gathered, was a reference to the arrest of representatives of the Student Nonviolent Coordinating Committee after a conference with Odinga in an Atlanta hotel room. I told Odinga I had been trying to see him for a week to talk about anti-Americanism in East Africa.

"Ha ha," Odinga said, "Oh, no! Come with me to watch the dancers!"

While a wondrous troupe of acrobatic Wakambas danced and

drummed, Odinga moved on. Later, he gave me a nod while talking to Bildad Kaggia, the Kikuyu politician with whom Odinga had made common cause in an effort to broaden his appeal. But he did not speak with me again.

In a rented car early next morning, as the sun arose somewhere out of sight and turned the mists a fresh pale blue, I drove in a caravan of journalists from Information House off Victoria Street to the site of the Seven Forks Hydroelectric development project on the Tana River about eighty-five miles northwest of Nairobi. Here, President Kenyatta was scheduled to preside over a dedication ceremony. I had one passenger, a Luo photographer named B'anda, who had spent a year learning his trade in West Berlin. He was a slight, taciturn young man dressed in patched clothing. He carried two cheap cameras in a scuffed camera bag. He looked hungry. I bought some chocolate in Thika on the main road to Nyeri, which considerably brightened B'anda's spirits. We turned off at Thika onto an unimproved road that ran two hours through desolate dry bush to the site. We saw few people and no animals. So, all that time, B'anda and I talked about life in Kenya. City life depressed him, he said, and would drive him back to the *shamba* (farm) if he did not find himself a girl pretty soon. After a fling in the modern world, Luos often return to Nyanza. B'anda said that the Luo believe in love-marriages but that the girl's family requires a dowry from the boy. "Usually cattle," B'anda said, "which are returned if there is a divorce." I told him it was not that much different in the States. B'anda laughed. He said he did not expect Kenya to achieve real unity because intermarriage among such tribes as the Luo and the Kikuyu could not be arranged. "It is simple," B'anda said. "They believe in female circumcision and we don't."

Nearing the site, we passed a tall Masai family marching along behind a herd of cows. They wore long earrings and purple gowns and carried shiny spears. "They are on the move all their lives," B'anda said. "Their marriages are arranged in infancy, but

they can exchange a wife or take one from another just by placing a spear in front of her hut. Try that in America!"

We arrived in a clearing on the banks of the Tana River. Low
brown hills topped with acacia trees surrounded us on all sides.
The entire valley would be flooded when the dam was built. I
parked among a tangle of jeeps and Land-Rovers, got out, and
waited for B'anda before hiking the last fifty yards to the ceremonial platform. But B'anda stayed on his side of the car. Overhead, the sky was blue-white and cloudless.

"Come on," I said.

"I see you later," B'anda said. "Thank you."

Then he walked on an angle toward the river bank where five
or six Africans were dozing in the shade of an ancient tree. I
thought I had made a friend—perhaps I had. But B'anda felt he
did not belong with me now.

Below the parking area, an honor-guard platoon of Kenya Police stood at attention. They wore red fezzes, brief khakis, and
high socks. A short, impossibly thin African martinet snapped a
command which brought their rifles forward for inspection. Behind him, a buck-toothed Englishman wearing the insignia of the
Kenya Police supervised the drill from underneath a campaign
hat with the brim pinned up on one side, Anzac-style.

Further along, members of a military band weighted down
with instruments and black-and-white wool uniforms sat in a circle under another shade tree. Then there was a long, green tent
with a bar and cafeteria tables inside where a dozen Africans in
shorts and clean T-shirts hopped about, slicing vegetables, wiping
dishes, and organizing the drinks under the violent dominion of
a German-speaking cook. And just beyond the tent, a gazebo
decked out in red-and-white bunting creaked and shook under a
horde of English and African technicians who were setting up
sound equipment for the festivities. The area swarmed with white
and black men, dignitaries, workers and the engineers responsible
for the project. I smoked a cigarette with a gray-haired farmer
dressed in Scotch tweeds. When I told him I was planning to
drive alone to Nyeri and Mt. Kenya for the weekend, he shook his

head. "You shouldn't drive alone," he said. "But let me warn you—if you accidentally hit an African on the highway, don't stop or you'll be mobbed. That's the way it is now."

Just then, a Mercedes drove into the site, past the parking lot and up to the edge of the luncheon tent. Jomo Kenyatta stepped out, a man well over seventy, with a large full stomach embraced by a beaded belt. He wore a red, yellow, and green fez on his graying head and carried both a carved ebony cane and a fly-whisk. The guard of honor marched into position near the gazebo. The guests stood beside chairs in the sun. Scores of Africans crowded a wire fence that ran along the site behind us. Across the river, several large families waved from a knoll. Kenyatta walked heavily to the gazebo, missing the beat of a brisk march blown on the wind by the military band. After six years in prison, he might never walk among the symbols of power without an air of irony, perhaps even boredom. The music stopped. Then there was a shrill, sweet, whistling sound—a respectful greeting from the un-invited Africans behind the fence. Kenyatta stepped into the gazebo and raised his flywhisk in salute as the band played Kenya's national anthem.

He spoke briefly about the need for economic development. Then there was more music, followed by a grand explosion—earth and water erupted into the sky above a bend in the river. The hydroelectric project had been dedicated with a small charge of TNT.

We fell upon our luncheon, a safari feast of cold chicken and pressed meat, salad, cheeses, and beer. Englishmen eagerly crowded around Kenyatta, who did not seem to enjoy their attentions. I did not see him again, either.

Without running over a single pedestrian on the highway, I drove up to Nyeri late that afternoon. B'anda had hitched a ride back to Nairobi with a TV crew. I spent Saturday evening at Treetops, a weekend tourists' game-watching hotel built in a stand of trees overlooking a waterhole. After midnight, a ghostly rhino tiptoed into view. At dawn, an elephant appeared. Meanwhile, there were steady visitations from wildebeests, water buffalo, warthogs, and baboons.

Sunday morning, I stopped in for tea at the home of an American Baptist missionary named Hull. As it happened, the reverend was off in Mweiga conducting a service, but Mrs. Hull, a bright, weathered lady, had her own view of anti-Americanism in Kenya. "The British are far worse than the Africans," she said. "They don't even like our *voices!* But mostly, they're leaving. There used to be six thousand civil servants, teachers, farmers, and shopkeepers in this area. But in the past eighteen months, perhaps five thousand or more have gone. It's the price of Africanization. Even the golf club is being taken over for farming. The British were opposed to our Baptist mission helping the Africans. Some of them were racists, believers in segregation who just despise Africans, so they despised us. . . . When we drove in here in 1959, the people thought we were British because our car was a Land-Rover. So, we were criticized. Then, when we explained that we were Americans, the Africans suspected us of ulterior motives. Now they see we mean to help them. They are mostly simple, friendly people—suspicious, as they have a right to be, but once you make a friend, he's a friend. If they're stirred up about America, most likely some politician is doing it. . . . See, they love to come out for big rallies. They will walk miles to come to a political rally. But, since they can't read, they will believe whatever a politician tells them, whether it's a lie or the truth about America. They are, of course, anti-*white*. But they can be pro-American or anti-American depending on what a politician they like says. The question to ask is why do politicians attack the United States? I would say it is because our image includes capitalism, exploitation, and segregation. Then, too, you can't rule out the possibility that some of the politicians are mercenaries. . . . Most of us say that the United States has put too much money in here. What Africans appreciate is people who work with them. I teach women how to cook. My husband works with them building churches and roads. People appreciate this. But sending money doesn't win friends. You don't love your rich uncle. When you give someone money without his having worked for it, you take away his sense of pride. If you put up a church for him, he doesn't take pride in it. But if you help him put up his own church, he appreciates it. That's what we've learned. . . . No, America should not pull out. But it would be worse to get thrown out. A delicate decision. It even affects my husband and me. We don't want to be dead heroes. We will stay here as long as there is no danger to us. If things become chaotic, we won't be able to help much until things settle down. A dead missionary is no good to anyone."

By noon, I had crossed the equator at an altitude of six thousand feet and could see the snows of Mt. Kenya ahead, another two miles up. I had lunch at the Mt. Kenya Safari Club, a little bit of old Grossinger's in darkest Africa partly owned by William Holden who was right there in the dining room having smorgasbord with Capucine. I met an Austrian at the bar who had given up farming for tourism since independence. He had a nicely unified view of the world. His interest was tourism, which meant saving the game from drought, disease, indiscriminate killing, and the encroachment of agricultural man on the game country. Conservation in Kenya, he said, depended on international interest and investment, which depended upon stable political and economic development in East Africa which, in turn, depended on world conditions, including the outcome in Vietnam! Everything, he said, depended on everything else.

Monday morning, I drove west around Aberdare National Park down into Nakuru in the heart of the great Rift valley. Here, on Lake Nakuru, there were hundreds of thousands of flamingos huddled together in enormous clumps that looked, from a distance, like great islands of pink coral. Calmly, they fed on the best-tasting algae (for flamingos) in the world. They were imperturbable. I was told nothing short of a cannon shot could move them unless they were ready to fly.

Then, after lunch with an old-timer who still remembered the first stone building in Nakuru—"some forty years ago, son"—I headed back toward Nairobi, one hundred miles down the road.

On the way, I passed the Nakuru-Nairobi train which makes the journey up mountains and through the savannah plain in nine hours. There were vast tea and coffee plantations and cattle ranches scattered in the valley, but most were invisible from the highway. What one saw were village clumps of mud huts that housed men whose grandparents had been strangers to the wheel. And barefooted children driving cattle across the road. And an overturned bus whose passengers, miraculously unharmed, patiently waited for the next one to come along. And an exquisite giraffe loping along in a cloud of dust. And everywhere the drought that had burned the earth the color of winter.

Tuesday, my last day in Nairobi, I had some luck. Three ministers decided to talk to me.

Early in the morning, there was Dr. Mjoroge Mungai, a Stanford-educated M.D., President Kenyatta's personal physician, and recently-appointed Minister of Defense. Mungai was in his early forties, handsome, articulate, and said to be one of Kenyatta's favorites in the successor sweepstakes. Counting heavily in his favor was one crucial fact: Mungai was a Kikuyu. He talked for more than an hour, occasionally punctuating a remark by shooting his cuffs. He was never less than smooth, attractive, and utterly unoriginal. I wanted to leave when he got around to how much he loved J.F.K. But the gist of his analysis was interesting. "How," he asked, "can America be involved with Africa on the technological and educational level without entanglement on the political level? The answer is sensitivity, which simply means you should not make it a condition that we should be friendly to you."

Next, I saw Ramogi Oneko, then Minister of Information in charge of both "Voice of Kenya," the government radio station, and the government controlled Kenya News Agency. Oneko had often identified himself with Oginga Odinga and other African leftists—he even appointed one of the few avowed communists in Kenya to run the news agency. But it was by no means clear whether he was pro-Russian, pro-Chinese, or simply pro-Oneko.

For example, after the Russians had supplied all sorts of equipment for the news agency, Oneko refused the Tass news service. At the same time, he was paying about forty thousand dollars a year for Reuters. When the Russians protested, Oneko agreed to accept Tass—but only if he did not have to pay for it. Then he ordered the Voice of Kenya and the local papers to use both services without identifying either! But in any case, it seemed that Oneko was thoroughly anti-American. He greeted me in his office with an aide standing by to make notes on our conversation. He was a tall, intense, middle-aged propagandist whose taste in furniture was limited to dark wood and red leather. On the wall hung a map, a zebra skin, and crossed spears.

"You like that?" he said.

"The zebra—very much," I replied.

"That's good. Sit down."

We sat facing each other across his desk, my back to the zebra. The aide sat on my left and never spoke.

"What can I do for you?" Oneko asked.

"Well, I'm interested in your thoughts on anti-Americanism."

"Are you?"

"Yes, sir."

"Well—!"

Oneko leaped from his chair, bounded around his desk, and seemed to be going for one of the spears. As he loped across the room, I saw a great hunter move for the kill. He scared the hell out of me. But when he reached the wall, he merely gave the map a whack with the flat of his hand.

"There!" he cried. "That is Kenya!"

I nodded, indubitably.

"The American had no interest in Kenya when the British government was in power."

I nodded again.

"But when it was known that the British were leaving, the United States became very keen about what was going on."

More nods.

"Oh, everyone was very happy about arranging the education

of our boys in the United States," Oneko said, as he reclaimed his desk seat. "But then, suddenly, when we started knowing more about what was going on in the United States in the way of discrimination, we began to have doubts."

"I can understand that, but—"

"We asked, 'If the Americans are serious, why segregation in America?'"

"We are trying to do something about it."

Oneko ignored me. He talked through me to *us*.

"One: the people of Kenya are very much concerned about the security of their country. Two: they are anxious to remain master of their own destiny."

"Aren't we all?"

"Your aid should not interfere with independence."

"Has it?"

"The British, who were masters here yesterday, are coming back offering friendship and we are very suspicious. If you had been quarreling with someone who ran off with your wife, and if he comes back and offers to help you look after your wife, you can't trust him, or his friend, can you?"

"We are not the British."

"You have almost the same ideology."

"No, we're quite different."

"Ha ha, so true! Wherever there is an American influence, they always try to suggest the sort of people to lead the country. They build up their choices financially and do not let the people decide alone. The British are more subtle and more sensitive. There must be a changed approach for U.S. diplomacy toward young nations. If we don't always agree with you, don't brand us communist or stupid bugger. The word communism is very emotional in America. But it is wrong to assume anyone who disagrees with you is a communist sympathizer."

"For example?"

"The Congo. I tell you Tshombe won't be there a year from now. Write down: March 9, 1966. Look it up in 1966." (Oneko was right; and by the fall of 1966, he himself was out of a job.)

"Perhaps we should leave Africa."

"You can't. You must choose whether to be with the majority of Africa or the minority that held the yoke."

"Withdrawal is being talked about a lot right now."

"Not from *Africa*. You can have influence through friendship."

"It doesn't seem to work very well, friendship."

"Ech! American journalists! They write home telling people in America that Africans love them. *No!* You are being misled. You must change your attitude worldwide. What happens in Vietnam is next door for all of us."

"I understand."

"No, Americans do not understand. America is big. But so is the elephant and he can be killed by the bee. When the bee flies up the trunk, the elephant beats the trunk on the ground and he falls."

Oneko grinned and led me to the door.

"But don't get me wrong," he said. "I like Bill Attwood."

Finally, mid-afternoon, I met the Minister of Justice, Tom Mboya. He arose from behind a big, clean desk and held out a beefy hand. Then he sat down on the edge of his chair, as though he only had a moment. He was round-faced and athletic-looking, age 34, dressed to the nines. He wore a carefully-tailored silk suit, one of scores reported in the closet at home in his big house in the suburbs. There was an emerald on his left pinky. His manner was sonorous, if not pompous, but he was cautious. Perhaps the worst that could have happened was that I should write something favorable about him. A pro-Mboya cover story on *Time* had once laid him open to charges of American influence and, for several seasons, tarnished his local image. At twenty-three Mboya had successfully led a dock strike in Mombasa. Thereafter, he was lionized by American labor leaders anxious to acclaim the rise of a liberal anti-colonialist in East Africa. Many touted Mboya, a Luo, as Kenyatta's leading rival. But after independence, Kenyatta emerged with such strength that Mboya could only fall back upon Justice, one of the lesser ministries in the government. For the past year, Mboya had been tend-ing to business. He was still young enough to let the future take care of itself. Mboya's discussion of anti-Americanism intrigued me for its absence of passion on any side—or rather, its concern for *both* sides. "Whereas African people express indignation toward America for propping up Tshombe," he said, "there are still areas of American activity in Africa that are fully appreciated. We continue to work on many A.I.D. projects. We have students in the States. We are discussing new programs. There is a positive side in our relations being marred by the Congo situation. . . . Anti-American demonstrations are a spontaneous reaction on the part of our people against external intervention in an African situation. . . . People think there is a parallel between Vietnam and the Congo. For us, Vietnam is a serious example of what happens when the United States intervenes in a small country. We fail to see how that small country has so many generals. It is comical. And for America to be involved in such a comedy is bound to undermine its position in the eyes of new nations. . . . I don't believe there is a trend toward anti-Americanism among students returning from the States. I would categorically say that is untrue. I want more students to go." With Mboya, one paid his money and took his choice.

As it turned out, Mboya had had only a moment—in less than half an hour, he interrupted himself, called his fragile English secretary, and arranged for my exit. Still remembering those days in New York when Mboya was the darling of the labor movement and of Americans for Democratic Action, to which I belonged, I was disappointed.

Yet, as I ambled along Government Road, I wondered what I had expected. Mboya was playing a waiting game, which included the politics of anti- and pro-Americanism. It was perhaps a measure of his shrewdness that for the time being he expressed a little of both.

I passed the United States Information Service Library, a small storefront with wall racks for books and magazines and eight tables with eight seats at each, all filled by young Kenyans. And on another street, a much larger crowd had gathered to go through a portable U.S.I.S. exhibit of life in America presented in a well-designed, airy little exposition building with Swahili-speaking Africans on hand to describe U.S. machinery, garden equipment, clothing, and health practices. With the exception of a special exhibit, entitled "The Negro American Moves Ahead," they were treated to a display that made emphatic use of white mannequins and photos using only white models.

7
Frenchmen

My landing in Paris at noon on March 10 was more than an arrival; it was a homecoming. In the past ten years as a tourist and working journalist, I had made half-a-dozen visits to France and lived there as long as three months at a time. I had seen the creeping Americanization of resurgent France, the gradual acceptance of drugstores, rock-and-roll, jeans, supermarkets, Parisian imitations of *Time* and *Playboy*, the TV series, housing projects, and much of the best in American art and literature. Most recently, in the early spring of 1962, I spent a month researching a *Look* article about Jean Monnet and the Common Market. Those were the days of J.F.K.'s "Grand Design," when Monnet's idea of an Atlantic Partnership between the United States and "Europe" seemed irresistible. But then de Gaulle spoiled it. In January 1963, he rejected Britain's nomination for membership in the Common Market and emphasized, as never before, his determination to end America's European "hegemony."

In the following two years, French anti-Americanism became our favorite example of man's ingratitude to man. We had been jilted by our mistress. France drained off our gold. France vetoed our color TV system while pushing its own. France refused to sign the nuclear test-ban treaty. France condemned our Vietnam policy. France threatened to expel American NATO troops. France criticized American investment in French businesses. France even refused permission for the opening of an American consulate in Tahiti. And, insultingly, de Gaulle himself refused to attend celebrations on the twentieth anniversary of D-Day, June 6, 1964.

Our side, of course, counterattacked. An appeal to "see America first" cut into the Paris-bound flow of tourist dollars. We teamed up with the West Germans to capture most of Western Europe for our color TV system. We refused to sell France any more enriched uranium. We made plans to shift our NATO forces into Germany. And we slowed down our investments. We got even, all right. But on balance, we played de Gaulle's game. It was clear by the late winter of 1965 that the United States, *as leader*, was less effectively involved in Europe than at any time since the war. No one wanted to admit it—Konrad Adenauer had created an uproar when he complained of America's "withdrawal" from Europe in an interview with C. L. Sulzberger of the New York *Times*. Still, the fact remained. The Russian *détente* made it increasingly difficult to justify our old policy, while concentration on our interests in Southeast Asia increasingly limited our chances of thinking up a new one. Presumably, we wanted to stay in Europe to make peace. But de Gaulle's anti-American policy was not-so-gently pushing us toward the door. I wanted to find out what I could about all this and, at the same time, try to find some answers for myself. My travels were almost over.

That first afternoon in Paris was sunny and cold—pretty good, but not yet spring. At my old hotel on Rue Mt. Thabor, M. Duminy gave me my favorite room under the eaves. He recalled the night in 1962 when we stood together by the kitchen radio, listening to de Gaulle's "My Dear France" speech that marked the beginning of the end in Algeria. Outside, twenty thousand police and guardsmen had been alerted for sabotage and even an attempted coup. The chef wept and the porter shook his fist. De Gaulle was truly grand that night.

I unpacked and went around the corner to say hello to my

friend, Simone Gauthier, at the *Look* office on Rue St. Honoré. Simone is a vivacious blonde who has mastered the art of Paris-bureau management for a foreign magazine. She knows French politics, *haute couture*, the art scene, the avant garde, and all the best restaurants in every price range. Besides, she is a five-star cook in her own right while her husband, an Icelandic linguist named Christopher Finbogassen, hoards fine wines in the cellar of their apartment house on the Left Bank. Simone is a student of human nature: one look at me told her I needed food. So that evening she cooked while Christopher and I sat in their tiny living room under a Braque and two Bomboises killing our taste buds with whisky and smoke. The cocktail hour has come to France at last, Christopher laughed. "When Americans drank before dinner," he said, "it was vulgar. Now that the French do it, it's *chic*." Simone served goose liver *pâté* with truffles for openers, followed by lamb in wine sauce, salad, and a soufflé, all prepared in less than an hour in her closet-sized kitchen. Afterwards, in the warmth of the dining room over a last glass of lovely wine, we agreed that anti-Americanism was a depressing subject.

"Only an American would study it," Simone said.

We laughed but the truth hurt.

"Americans want to be popular," she continued. "It is not a terrible disease."

"But it should be cured," I said, tentatively.

"No, the problem is how to live."

Marlow said almost exactly that to Stein in *Lord Jim*.

During two of the next three weeks, I talked to some twenty Frenchmen representing a wide range of Parisian opinion. Among them were government officials, businessmen, journalists, soldiers, and artists. Between times, I vacationed with my wife, Joan, who had flown over to Paris on the proceeds of the *Life* article about Sukarno. We even spent five days with friends on a farm in Scotland and visited London, which shall be beyond the scope of this chronicle. I relaxed for the first time in four months. But also, I found myself listening to people in a new way because of Simone's remark after dinner that first night. The truth was that all the discussions I had around the world were about how to live. They mattered, not because they were right or wrong, but because they dealt with this problem. America, I decided, had been thinking alone too long. We suffered a new kind of isolationism—the isolation of the Most Powerful. It deprived us of a priceless lode of world experience.

My first interview, a few days after the dinner with Simone and Christopher, was in the offices of *Le Monde*, a first-rate daily newspaper representing the democratic center in France, on Rue des Italiens. Here I met Claude Julien, a dapper writer with the title of assistant foreign editor, who had a substantial reputation for fairness and perception. He showed me to his desk, where I asked him whether he thought anti-Americanism was good politics for de Gaulle. Julien smiled. He said foreign policy and American investments in France were the two main factors in the politics of anti-Americanism. "De Gaulle does not miss one opportunity to criticize United States policy," he said, "but to my mind, this is not done systematically. De Gaulle is not exploiting an anti-American feeling. Rather, when he disagrees with you, he gives way to nationalism. I am convinced millions of average, moderate Frenchmen follow him in this. This is the great middle group of people who are not extremists but who resent American strength. They are nationalists. They want France to be a big, powerful country and resent very strongly American might. I believe this is clear. Look at the difference in French opinion after 1918 and after 1945. We had pride after 1918, because we had won. After 1945, we felt humiliated. This has a very important effect on our attitudes."

"But France cannot be a *big* power," I said.

"Without the handicap of Indochina and Algeria, de Gaulle wants to lead France to international power. It has to do with our self-conception. Georges Bidault in San Francisco at the United Nations meeting, 1945, had a conversation with some Americans who were worried that France would try to lead the small nations of the world against the United States and Russia. 'Don't worry,' said Bidault, 'France is too big a country to become the leader of a union to protect small countries.'"

"Doesn't this play into the hands of the communists?"

"The extreme left is routinely anti-American, of course. But this means little now. The Communist Party has lost much power. We had a referendum not long ago in which one million normally leftist votes went for de Gaulle. They still have good propaganda because you are in Vietnam, and they exploit it. But they have had to close up their newspapers in the provinces and the circulation of *L'Humanité*, their Paris paper, is down from 400,000 in 1941 to 100,000 today. Oddly, they will criticize de Gaulle's domestic policy but they support his anti-American diplomacy because it is against the United States. The fact is that the left generally supports de Gaulle's diplomacy and also the center—academics, professionals, and business people who are the basis of the old nationalistic French opinion. They love French art, French food, Brigitte Bardot—France, France, France! They do not agree with Jean Paul Sartre, but they are proud that he is a Frenchman. De Gaulle appeals to all those obscure feelings in these people.

"Do not overestimate anti-Americanism in France, however. Many Frenchmen are criticizing your policy in Vietnam not because of anti-Americanism but because of logic. We tried your policy in Vietnam for nine years and lost."

"You don't disagree with what we're trying to do?"

"We appreciate the domino theory, but the way you are reacting to it seems wrong to us. Air strikes must be accompanied with a peace plan."

"President Johnson says he wants to negotiate peace."

"A plan is something more and, without one, it is difficult for Frenchmen to give L.B.J. the benefit of the doubt. Now, de Gaulle has proposed neutralization of the area. This is not an anti-American proposal. It was not put forward to humiliate the United States. Rather, its purpose was to enhance de Gaulle's own image as a peacemaker and his reputation for foresight. He wanted to suggest that he has the power to get the United States and China to listen to him."

Julien paused for the cigarette ritual.

"The other point," he said, "is the flow of American money into

Europe. Businessmen are not patriots. They want to make money. If they can make it off the United States, okay. Or China. But—do you know about the Machine Bull episode?"

I said I did. Bull, France's largest electronic company, recently had been taken over by General Electric after French money failed to rescue it from financial straits.

"The newspapers criticized de Gaulle for surrendering Bull to the United States," Julien said. "Noncommunist-left papers and some right papers used this to show contradictions in de Gaulle's policy. A lot of people interpreted this as anti-Americanism, but there was a strong element of anti-Gaullism, too."

"Well, is it dangerous?" I asked.

"Personally, I don't think so. Many people here are enthusiastic about America and American culture. Personal relations are good. What is happening is that de Gaulle is increasing French chauvinism to help the morale. . . . After the war, when the great majority of people had no reactions to anything, there was no French diplomacy. Then during the Indochina war and the Algerian war, we needed American assistance and the Marshall Plan, so we could not criticize. Our foreign ministers were so afraid of losing your support that they would do anything to please your State Department. This, of course, led to the miscalculations about the European Army plan in 1956. Mendès-France got blamed for killing it, because our diplomats had told the State Department what you wanted to hear—that there was support in the French Assembly for a European Army. Actually, there was never a chance. . . . In those days, the pendulum had swung too far toward the United States. Now it has gone too far the other way. But it will come back again. When de Gaulle disappears, someone like Gaston Defrerre will be President, a man who would never dare be as blunt as de Gaulle."

"It seems," I said, "that we are most popular when France has wars to fight and needs money—"

"Some Americans might say France is ungrateful."

"Some *might!*"

"But this is the way it is all over the world. The Russians have the same trouble dealing with the Roumanians. It is the problem of a big country dealing with a small country that used to be big. France feels, on the one hand, that America is so big it does not need French help and, on the other hand, that it is only natural to go to the United States for help in time of need."

"Americans find that hard to understand."

"Our countries are very nationalistic. We each see things our own way. The United States accuses de Gaulle of trying to break up the Atlantic alliance. But de Gaulle disagrees. He says he is trying to strengthen the Atlantic alliance on a basis that would give more of a voice to France. Or consider this: It is impossible for you to renounce your monopoly of atomic power. But it is also impossible for France, a smaller country, to rely on the American decision in this matter. It is the Left here in France that criticizes de Gaulle's *force de frappe,* and yet these are the most anti-American Frenchmen. These are the people who do not trust you to protect us in an atomic war. Thus, de Gaulle makes political capital on the Left with his anti-Americanism and, at the same time, takes the stinger out of the leftists who are opposed to his *force de frappe. . . .* Conversely, the rightists might oppose aspects of de Gaulle's foreign policy, but they get the domestic order they like. They even like recognition of Red China because it constitutes a business opportunity."

"In short, he makes a stew out of French politics."

"Exactly! De Gaulle's aim is to keep himself in power, to make himself a big man. And in the process, he has succeeded in breaking up the traditional political alignments of France. I say this has been a great service because our political parties showed they could not solve our problems. For example, they could not disengage from Algeria, but de Gaulle did it. They could not have maintained cooperation with Algeria, but de Gaulle has done that, too. The man is not a nationalist, he is a Gaullist. He sees France through his own eyes."

Next day, to talk to a journalist who had consistently backed de Gaulle, I sought out Maurice Delarue, chief diplomatic correspondent of *France-Soir*, a daily managed in the Hearst style by one Pierre Lazareff. I arrived at Delarue's office on Rue Reaumur late in the afternoon, catching him just as he was leaving for the day. Slight, dark, and wearing a tight blue suit, he suggested we continue in a bar down the street. As we walked along the sidewalk, jostled by crowds of clerks and shopgirls heading home with their breadsticks, Delarue told me he felt de Gaulle's foreign policy was right, but his manners were very bad. The crowd buffeted us at that moment, and Delarue smiled dryly at me. Then in the safety of a workingman's bar, the rear of which offered three varieties of pinball, we ordered an *apéritif*. Delarue, like Claude Julien, had an orderly mind. He said there were three points to de Gaulle's policy and denied that any of them were directed against the United States. The first was nationalism. The second was "Europe." And the third was the Atlantic alliance. "De Gaulle," he said, "thinks the nation is the basis of any society. There are states that never become real nations with their own personality, history, and territory. These disappear, while those states that are nations, regardless of size, will survive. So, starting from this basis of nation-ness. he believes the nations closest to France geographically are most important to France. That means Germany, especially. Then he wants to create a united Europe, step by step giving it a national philosophy and consciousness. . . . Finally, he believes this Europe should be allied to the United States."

"Where does Great Britain fit in?"

"De Gaulle would want them out of Europe, but allied to it along with their Commonwealth. But if they want to go into Europe, he could not turn them down."

"And Russia?"

"Ultimately, de Gaulle hopes for a reconciliation of all Europe, based on the probable evolution of all, East and West. You know, France is not completely capitalist itself. We have nationalized medicine, industries, railroads, and schools. We pay a government salary bonus to all wage earners. We are, thus, not that different from Eastern European countries. De Gaulle feels all the regimes of Europe are growing more alike. It will be a long, slow process. But, in any case, de Gaulle does not see a communist problem in the world now. It is a fact that nationalism is stronger than communism, which is an internal problem for the communist countries. What de Gaulle sees is a larger community of all Europe with Germany contained as a part of it."

"How would it happen?" I asked.

"Only if there is, first, an independent, nuclear, united Western Europe, followed by the evolution of Eastern Europe and East Germany into this union. If it happens, this reconciliation will not be anti-American, for there will be no more Cold War. It will be a reconciliation of the white people of the world."

"The *white* people?"

Delarue had spoken so blandly that I thought I had misunderstood. But there was no doubt that the factor of race was decisive in his interpretation of Gaullism.

"The white people of the world," he said.

I thought of Vietnam and my own ambiguous feelings about our involvement there. The argument that we did not *belong* in Southeast Asia had always seemed to me to be touched with this sort of racism.

Delarue seemed to read my mind. "We are not against America's Vietnam policy because we are anti-American. We are against it because this policy will never succeed. France did the same there and in North Africa when the old-style nationalists were in charge. The Vietnamese people cannot become anticommunist when their children are being killed. The people in the villages were anti-communist but now they become communist. Some day the Americans will leave and, having waged this kind of war, you will leave all these people as communists. The problem is political, not military, and can only be settled by discussion."

"We cannot pull out," I said.

"De Gaulle does not say pull out. He says that if you use military means, you must also show the people a peaceful way out. You must propose something besides unconditional surrender

—something like neutralization, as de Gaulle has said. But it is not that he took this view just to annoy you. No. Rather, he thinks it is a dangerous policy and, also, he does not want France to be driven out of Vietnam. The French have a secondary school in Hanoi. Many Vietnamese students study here in Paris. We cannot be indifferent when we have these cultural ties."

Not to mention rubber plantations and the like.

After a week or so in Paris, I realized that high government officials would be even more difficult to see than their counterparts in Kenya. Minister of Finance Valéry Giscard d'Estaing and Foreign Minister Couve de Murville, whom I had particularly wanted to meet, were under orders to speak publicly only on pertinent matters of state.

At Giscard d'Estaing's office on Rue de Rivoli, a young member of the staff had kindly undertaken to explain to me French economic policy toward the United States in regard to gold and investments. Dressed in black flannels, he maintained that, politics aside, there was some uncertainty about the dollar reflected in the increasing desire of dollar-holders to buy gold. The uncertainty, he said, arose from America's international deficit which had to be corrected either by reducing its foreign military commitments and economic aid or by restricting its investments abroad. Only the latter seemed desirable, but thus far American efforts in this direction had not been sufficient. Therefore France sought to reform the international monetary system before it was too late. "You can imagine my personal views and the government's," the young man said, meaning to tell me that he and Giscard did not support de Gaulle's idea of returning to the gold standard, but that they did indeed want the United States to attack its deficit.

Couve de Murville's man at the Quai d'Orsay had been equally polite as he denied me an audience with his minister. Appropriately, he wore pin stripes and a double-breasted vest, and smartly summarized for me the official line: France was the naughty boy of the Atlantic alliance, he said, because it sought more responsibility for "Europe." He contended there were no anti-Americans in France except for a few bloody fools and highly cultured types who took exception to the Americanization of Europe. "We like having Libby's here," he said, "because you Americans know how to *can* food better than we do. . . ."

And at the Élysée Palace, another gentleman in black flannel had expressed regrets that President de Gaulle was so busy. He assured me, however, that the basic Franco-American friendship was not to be questioned. The difference was that normalcy had returned, and Europeans, led by France, had a feeling of greater independence. "It is not random or by chance," he said, "that signs of this difference are occurring all at once. You do not misunderstand us. A new position has been taken. We want to put you Americans in your place. Ours is a calculated policy necessary for the survival of France and Europe."

The one exception to all this good-natured indifference was Minister of Information Alain Peyrefitte, whose job required daily contact with the press. He could talk to me, but not for quotation. And as I expected, he denied any taint of prejudice against us. Peyrefitte, however, had been Minister of Information since 1962 when his appointment was viewed as a reflection of an intensified anti-American or, as the Gaullists insisted, pro-French policy. Under his supervision, General France Television, the government TV monopoly, showed greater ambivalence toward America than ever before: Most nights, it featured in prime time *Bonanza, The Untouchables,* and other U.S. programs. Like American films, such programs were more than entertainment; they were information. The French took our Westerns seriously and did not always understand that *The Untouchables* was historical fiction. But the net effect was probably "affirmative." On the other hand, G.F.T. showed an increasing volume of news film that was decidedly unflattering to the United States. Ironically, American networks and news agencies supplied most of the footage on Vietnam and racial violence in the South, the two most popular subjects of the day, and most of it was devastating. Jacques Dupont, executive director of G.F.T., had told me, for example, that he felt President Johnson's recent "We Shall Overcome" speech had "balanced" the impact of daily scenes of brutality and terror in Selma, Alabama. But my impression was that the selection of news from U.S. sources was largely disagreeable. Moreover, there was little film of any kind from the East. One was then thrown back on his own political opinions to determine whether or not, beyond Gaullist malice, we deserved it. Having been away so long, I felt the homesick patriot's sense of outrage at both M. Peyrefitte and the syndication procedures of our dimwitted networks.

Our own people at the American Embassy on Avenue Gabriel were making the best of things. Their official point of view had it that it was totally wrong to say de Gaulle was anti-American. His policy, they said, simply reflected certain understandable policy disagreements. In this spirit, Nicholas King, the press attache, told me that he had never seen less evidence of anti-Americanism in France than at this time. "I don't think anyone dislikes the Americans," he said. "The French find American tourists have become self-effacing. It's the Germans who are loud and vulgar now, so everyone hates them. Also, the French who visit America are almost always terrifically impressed. And, finally, they are always against their own government. De Gaulle actually worries the man in the street with his antagonism toward the United States—you'll find Opposition politicians favoring NATO and being pro-American to attack de Gaulle."

Across the street, however, in the bar at the Hotel Crillon, American and British "observers" made observations of greater depth. I talked to one of each there late one day while waiting for Joan to return from a shopping tour on Faubourg St. Honoré. The American was a politically liberal syndicated newspaper correspondent. The Englishman worked on intelligence and other matters at the British Embassy. Neither would very much like to see his name here, so I shall call them Sam and John, respectively. We had been chatting about the Oxford-Cambridge boat race, won a few days earlier by Oxford with a crew including several

Americans, and this led John, the Englishman, to consider French attitudes toward people who speak English.

"The French see themselves as a unique civilization," he said. "The English language, spoken by you or us, and the technology represented by the United States threaten them. They fear you will cause them to lose their identity, and make them fail to achieve their goals. That's what's behind the Machine Bull controversy. They hate it that their own electronic industry can't get off the ground. They have a visceral feeling about it based on a badly informed image of America. They still have the prewar view of barbarous, vulgar America, a way station on the *Journey to the End of Night*. They can't believe America has great universities, because they've always believed that French is best. Going back to World War I, they cannot find fault with anything that France has done. They cannot see the other point of view at all. A Frenchman never puts himself in another chap's shoes."

"You wouldn't say anti-Americanism was virulent here, would you?" Sam asked. "In Athens and Ankara on the same day last year, the U.S. ambassador was hanged in effigy. The Greeks and the Turks have given up on us. We have exhausted our capital. But in France, among the people, I think there is a great reserve of love because of World War II."

"The important thing to keep separate is anti-Americanism on the diplomatic level, where there is a lot, and anti-Americanism on the grass-roots level, where there is little," John replied. "Frenchmen do complain about Americans to us British. They think the British submit to American pressure at every turn when, in fact, we're perfectly capable of muffing things by ourselves. This shows how close to the surface is their fear and lack of understanding of America."

With a fresh martini in hand, Sam said, "I see anti-Americanism as a political weapon. The French politician uses it to put the blame for his own shortcomings on an external force. It would be the same if, in the United States, we blamed poverty on the Russians. . . . Well, what to me is the terrible thing in France is that the worst right-wing reactionaries are often loudly pro-

American. Likewise in England, the conservative extremists support us. The world is everywhere more left than America."

"Left, but not necessarily liberal," John said, smiling.

"I stand corrected. But even so, the sensitive liberal has been alienated from government in the United States. We've had to pay for this."

John did not comment. He was concerned with the broader spectrum of French response to the United States. "For the next two or three years," he said, "or longer, perhaps, all that matters diplomatically is what de Gaulle thinks. He will make all policy in relation to the United States. He *wants* to differ from the United States. To him, an independent policy means a policy contrary to the United States. At the same time, there will be months when he attempts to camouflage this policy to quiet both his opposition and the British—both of whom think in terms of a partnership with the United States. They will charge de Gaulle with isolating France, so he will take steps to show that France is not isolated. But then he will campaign again against the United States. That's de Gaulle."

"He wants to die as a man without an enemy," Sam said. "He seeks *rapprochement* with everyone even if it means lowering his friends."

"I would call it a double ploy. First of all, he mystifies people so that no one knows what his real policy is, although it usually turns out to be anti-American and anti-British. Secondly, he always has a kernel of truth in what he says. The French are really more insular than the English, more selfish, too. They like de Gaulle's idea of *grandeur,* which restores the confidence they lost after the war, Dienbienphu, and Suez. Really, I do not believe there is such a thing as Gaullism. It is only a technique for realizing vague ideas that exploit psychological necessities of the French people on which de Gaulle rides high."

"France is more than de Gaulle—"

"I should say so," John continued. "France is this way. The French had no *anguish* over Suez. The British did. The French, if they think they are right, do not suffer from moral compulsions as we do. A Frenchman would never have the guilt complex found in Anglo-Saxons. Thus, it is easier to strike chords among them in terms of national pride and destiny."

Just then Joan came into the Crillon with a new hairdo and several boxes. Shopping agreed with her. She looked happy. John turned to the bartender and asked him in French if he was pro- or anti-American.

"Pro," the bartender smiled.

"You see!" John said, "I used to think General de Gaulle was only pro-France and could not really be anti-American, except indirectly. But with his policy of growth for France, I think he found America was in his way at every turn. For a time, anti-Americanism was not primary. But today, I believe he regards the reduction of American interference as his prime motive."

"Perhaps no one is anti-American except the politicians," Sam said.

"Well," John replied, "America is having its Elizabethan era and is bound to irritate everyone who is weaker."

April bloomed in Paris. From the Place de la Concorde, budding trees in the Tuileries gardens looked like an idea by Seurat. Manet's colors softened the soot-gray landscape on the Champs Élysées. Oysters were in season. I decided to stay for an extra week, hoping for some flash of insight that would illuminate all the scattered impressions of my trip. I had seen something of the tumult and complexity of the world, but I yearned for a point of view that could encompass it.

My search continued at lunch April 2, with a communist named Champsavior. He was a dry, tobacco-stained wretch who had been an editor at *Libération* before it folded for lack of communists. He was the kind of anti-American some Americans would like all anti-Americans to be. He spat when he mentioned our name. "U.S. politics," he said, "are too much based on militarism and economics, not enough on man's soul. America has no culture, eh? Hah! The Russians have Chekhov. The English have Shakespeare. The French have Voltaire and the Americans have Mickey Spillane."

I could not help teasing him. "You're forgetting *Bonanza,*" I said.

"You know," he replied, "I don't mind that."

Champsavoir was outraged by the bombing since February in North Vietnam.

"You will never get away with it!" he cried, as his oysters arrived—one dozen *fins de clare* on the half shell.

"We assume North Vietnam can stop the war at will," I said.

"No, you will not let them stop."

"Well, suppose our secret aim is to justify an attack on China's atomic installations, then what?"

"I tell you, M. Morgan, should this happen, there will be guerrilla warfare in Europe."

Next day, I looked up General Pierre Billotte, who lived in a fashionable neighborhood on the Right Bank. In 1962, de Gaulle appointed him chairman of the committee of the French Assembly on Franco-American friendship, presumably because he was a staunch UNR Gaullist and less well-disposed toward the United States than the previous chairwoman, Madame Thome-Pâtenotre. During World War II, he had been de Gaulle's chief of staff in London. Billotte greeted me in his foyer and led me into a den full of books and war trophies. He was a stocky, stiff-backed man in his sixties, a prototype of the aging professional soldier. At first sight, he reminded me that de Gaulle, *too,* was of that breed. They were bound to think of world politics as the province of strategy. I told Billotte what little I knew of French geopolitical theory. I understood that one of its key premises was China's alleged interest in Mongolia, Siberia, and other northern territory, which led Peking to seek a *cordon sanitaire* in Southeast Asia. If the United States were to withdraw from the south, the theory proposed, then China would turn north to put pressure on the Soviet Union. Conversely, the theory suggested that U.S. escalation in Vietnam would force Russia and China together in competition for the rest of the Red world. At some point, this would mean a Russian move, perhaps against West Berlin. Thus, in the

French view, nothing could be more dangerous than the present American policy. Billotte listened, eyes half-closed behind gold-rimmed glasses, occasionally nodding as I spoke. He was not, however, going to be led.

"That is the philosophy of M. Chauvel," he said and then launched his own discussion with only passing reference to the China-faces-north idea.

"Fundamentally," he said, "France and the United States share the same views. We are the same civilization and must defend the same values in the event of great danger. Ours are the only two nations in the West that have not warred against one another. But in the past few years, we've differed on details because the world has changed. There was the death of Stalin and the rise of Khrushchev. The growth of political as well as ideological differences between Russia and China. The loss of colonies by Great Britain and France. Finally, there was the recovery of Europe, the recovery of our sovereignty and our sense of responsibility. Thus, we have a brand new polycentric situation. And we feel that America has not paid attention to these changes."

General Billotte paused for a moment, as though weighing his next sentence. Then he winced and plunged ahead.

"Also," he confessed, "France has an inferiority complex. You must know this and expect it to be expressed in aggressiveness. We feel we have more experience in certain areas of foreign relations. We would like our views discussed. We feel you do not discuss with us your views on global strategy and so forth. On the contrary, when you do talk to us it is to prevent us from taking a decision. Thus, de Gaulle is probably your most difficult ally because he feels France has great experience and should be heard. Today, he is the only one like this in Europe. But, if Harold Wilson solves his problems, England will become as difficult as France. . . . You should prefer, but you don't, a strong ally who is difficult to deal with to a weak ally who is easy to talk to. This is the way it was during World War II. Your State Department preferred to talk to Bidault and Pétain, who were easy, rather than de Gaulle, who was difficult. So, in the context of this situation, there are the issues of the Atlantic alliance, disarmament, gold, Vietnam, tariffs, and East-West relations."

"Let's consider Vietnam," I said.

"I agree. President Johnson has just said for the first time that the United States wants to negotiate in Vietnam. And he has reaffirmed the necessity of South Vietnamese people to choose their own government. We appreciate the difficulty of your problem, but we can help. You don't realize that the French have recovered much influence in Vietnam."

Perhaps I did not realize it because there was so little evidence of it. But I did not want to interrupt. General Billotte continued:

"It is a difficult issue, but it cannot be solved without a global view. It must involve China, Cambodia, Russia, or else, even without a nuclear war, your present policy will perpetuate Chinese hostility. You need a global view worked out with the English and French and even the Russians. But, unfortunately, there has been no real consultation between the British, the French, and the Americans. You have not developed, as you might, flexibility toward the Russians. If you did, the North Vietnamese would be more ready to say they are willing to negotiate despite pressure from China.

"You must, through the British and the French, and then directly, involve the Russians and, finally, many people in Vietnam on your side. Surprisingly, perhaps, the French have good relations with Vietnamese in Hanoi, among Buddhists, and among military men. You could use this, but it is not being used because there are no precise relations between the United States and France. Your weakness is that you think you can deal with all problems by yourself and, therefore, you do not use all your assets. Even in North Vietnam, people with apolitical minds do not want the United States to withdraw *too* far! They want the Seventh Fleet to stay, they want you to remain in Thailand because they are always looking for ways to remain independent of China.

"You must not lose face. No Atlantic-minded Frenchman wants you to lose face. We want you to find a new solution. . . . It is now so totally stupid, what is going on. China's main interest is in Siberia and Manchuria. I agree with Chauvel on that. The Chinese want to create bad relations between the Americans and the Russians. And the Russians, who do not like the Chinese, do not want to seem traitors before the communist world. So because it puts the Russians on the spot, escalation is stupid. The Russians already envision a hundred years of war with China. And yet pressures from the communist parties around the world push Russia together with China because of Vietnam. It is totally stupid, when much closer talks with the British and the French could involve the Russians for you vis-à-vis blowing up the Chinese nuclear plant."

"For *us?*" I cried, suddenly finding myself in a scene from Dr. Strangelove. Newspapers had recently speculated on an American effort to destroy China's six-months'-old nuclear capability, but it seemed so incredible that I had not hesitated to tease Champsavoir with it. Now, however, in a confidential tone, Billotte was stating the prospect as a proposition.

"Let me tell you an anecdote, M. Morgan," he said. "Four days after the first Chinese atomic explosion, the British ambassador and the Russian ambassador to France were here in my house. We talked about what could be done. One suggested disarmament, but this is impossible. Then I suggested that the Russians bomb the Chinese installations. The Russian said, 'We could not.' Then I suggested, 'Let the Americans do it.' And the Russian said that might be possible. But there have been no talks since. You see, you have thought too much in terms of solving all problems yourselves or between yourselves and the Russians. It would help were you to collaborate with de Gaulle because, M. Morgan, the world has changed."

I got another perspective on all this from an unexpected source. A film director named Jean Aurel invited my wife and me for dinner the evening of the same day I talked with Billotte. With Jean, an old friend, I looked forward to a conversational mix of philosophy, art, and gossip according to the pattern we had long since established. He was a gangling, enthusiastic bachelor in his thirties with one exceptional film to his credit—*On Love*, a grayish-black humorous series of vignettes, in the mood of Stendhal set against the background of contemporary Paris. Politically, he had an anarchist's heart dominated by a conservative's brain. But he also had taste, which made him independent of all labels.

At eight that night, he picked us up at the Duminy and drove to a restaurant somewhere back of the Champs Élysées. The main course was an enormous pike that made a meal for the three of us. Afterwards, over coffee, Jean told us about his latest film, a documentary on World War I. He bragged that his research had made him an amateur military strategist. And, of course, his strategic viewpoints were cast to suit his rightist sympathies. Nevertheless, he used words in a way that forced me to reexamine even my liberalism. "America," Jean said, "had no strategy in 1918, and it has no strategy today because it has power, but no identity. America should admit that it is a racist, imperialist country, or else forget about power. The Russians are clearly racist. So are the Chinese. The Russians, finally, can get along with the Americans because, to them, China is a greater peril. If America understood the world, the Russians might be moved into a deal that gave them the upper hand in North Vietnam in exchange for tolerating an American attack on the Chinese A-bomb plants. But I doubt you can ever do the deed—we'll all regret it someday if you don't—because America has no way to communicate with the Russians. So, the British will go into Europe and learn again to compete and find an outlet for their Kipling-James Bond love of intrigue, this time against the French for dominance of the Common Market. And the Americans will be increasingly alone in the world, ruling according to their own version of imperialism, waiting for the Chinese."

"Jean, you're crazier than General Billotte," I said, knowing I would have to do better than that.

"Well, it is your dilemma," he said, waving his hands, "it is your dilemma! How to be leftist in domestic affairs and rightist in foreign affairs—that is, always realistic."

"The realists are always in power and then the war comes."

Jean made a sour face. "Listen, my friend, the goal is *to be!* You have been asking Frenchmen to tell you the truth about anti-Americanism, and they won't because they simply don't care about it—"

"The truth is a lot to ask. But I learned that as long as de Gaulle is President he will stir up anti-American feeling and try to separate us from Europe."

"Yes, but do you know why?"

"*Grandeur.*"

"Give him more credit. The French do not care about anti-Americanism, but they resent that the United States does not use its power to preserve life. You have to decide whether you want justice or liberty. You can't have both. Camus wanted both, but today we emphasize his 'witness for freedom'."

"We're trying to have both—I hope sincerely."

"It is nothing to be sincere. The test of one's intentions is the rightness of action."

"We're trying."

"Are you sure? Until America herself was threatened, she lectured everyone on morality and sought love. Now she is not preaching so much. She is doing in Vietnam exactly what she told us was wrong in 1954. Her policy has been hypocritical for forty years. Now she is not preaching so much and is less interested in being loved."

"We are very interested in prestige. I think I liked us better when love was all we wanted."

"But this is not the point. It is important to know the possibilities and the risks. Let me tell you the truth about the French. The French do not really like anybody but the French. Ask them what they think of the British or the Swiss or the Germans. Ugh! But the French are not dumb. They appreciate the United States' nuclear shield. They are also anti-government. So, it is this-minus-that. The ability to act alone makes you subject to special antago-

nism. We are worried you might move against China without
Russian consent. We are worried that your American troops have
been sent into Vietnam to draw an attack. But the Chinese are
probably too smart for that. Anyway, you have to see that we are
concerned because we love France. The French never leave
France because they think no place could be better. There is no
'brain drain' in France. Only the worst Frenchmen leave France.
The British used to send their very best to the colonies because
the oldest son, under their system, inherited everything and the
good young ones had to go out to make their way. Not so, the
French. We sent our worst to the colonies. All this says we are
concerned because we love France and our lives depend on a
President we can't vote for."

"You are saying anti-Americanism is not a real theme."

"*Mon cher,* it is a very nice excuse for traveling around the
world."

"I have to write a book."

"A book! It can be a great success if it is *funny!* See the humor
in an American, only an American, traveling around the world
wanting to be loved. It is not natural for men even to love their
wives, so why should they love Americans?"

"Jean!" my wife cried.

"Not you, my dear. Except for you."

"How do the French feel about the feelings of others toward
them?" I asked, doggedly.

"The French had all the power in the Twenties. . . . We were
hated. . . . We couldn't have cared less. People hate anyone with
the power to act alone. The humor is that all these people would
like to have that power."

"Very funny."

"Oh, yes. It is *very* funny. I see humor in it—the American
journalist takes the grand tour to find out why he is not loved
when, in fact, he has no reason to expect love and, as it turns out,
he finds that he *is* loved. I am French and I love you. It is thus
impossible for you to write that Americans are not loved in
France."

My wife flew home next day and I planned to follow as soon as I saw Jean Monnet. He had been in Brussels and London and was expected momentarily. On Friday afternoon, April 9, we finally got together at his office-apartment on Avenue Foch not far from NATO headquarters. I am a Monnet enthusiast; in 1962, I had been particularly impressed by his theory of change: "What, after all, is the process of civilization?" he had asked himself. "It is that, as material conditions create a need, men submit to new rules and institutions that they agree will govern them. The rules do not change human nature. But when men submit to the same rules, their behavior toward each other changes. Then they release new energy, and they begin to create interests in common. Problems that once seemed insoluble just disappear." Needless to say, Monnet was no Gaullist, but he was French or, rather, European. He would have a simple answer for anti-Americanism and many more important questions: create a *Europe* able to compare with the United States.

He greeted me in the large room off the front hall overlooking the avenue. Bookshelves lined three walls; his desk, a long table with papers precisely arranged, paralleled the fourth. In the two years that had passed, neither the room nor Monnet had changed. At seventy-five, he was the same short, trim burgher with clear blue eyes and fair skin, delicate hands and a soft voice. He wore a blue suit and a blue sweater and carried his reading glasses. He sat in a straight chair while I sank down in the old couch. I knew he did not have much time for interviews.

"Well," he said, "it is good to see you again, Mr. Morgan. I understand you've just traveled around the world."

"Almost."

"And you've been studying American policy. Tell me—what was the most important single thing you learned?"

I had thought I would have some months back in New York to think about that one question. It was no use talking about details or trying to sum up in a sentence. What I had learned was how little I knew.

"In every country I visited," I said, "almost no one felt confident about American foreign policy. We seem to have become something new in the world—a super isolationist power."

Monnet nodded, not sitting in judgment, but confident of his reply. He was a man with a grand idea, grander than most, that came as close as any I knew to embracing both the more developed and the less developed nations of the world.

"Now what is the question?" he asked, gently.

I thought of my favorite of all Gertrude Stein stories. On her death bed, she is asked, "Gertrude, what is the answer?" And her last words are, "What is the question?"

"The question is," I said, "What is our responsibility?"

Monnet nodded again. "The less developed countries complain about a lack of American policy because they want to know what the United States is going to give them," he said. "America is the leader and is expected to give. When it does not make up its mind, these countries accuse it of 'no policy.' The more developed countries are in transition. German elections are coming up. There is the British economic problem. By this fall or early in 1966, all this is going to be more clarified. President Johnson will then need to consider what are the problems and develop a world philosophy. He is a man of action and people are unclear about the meaning of his actions, but he is doing the best he can. When the time comes, he will be expected to develop not a policy, but a philosophy. Before World War II, your philosophy was *isolation*. England, France, and Germany had a philosophy then, too. It was *domination*. The British and the French convinced themselves that they were bringing *civilization* to their colonies, but their real purpose was to dominate. This is no longer possible. Now Vietnam does not make anyone too happy, but this, too, will be clarified this year. And then you will begin to develop a philosophy."

"But what philosophy?" I asked, hoping for a magic word.

"*Partnership*," Monnet said. "Partnership will be the only philosophy, as it was for President Kennedy. . . ."

Going away, I stopped late that afternoon at an apartment house a few doors from the Dome. On the top floor was Eugene Ionesco's apartment. Simone and Christopher Finbogassen had arrived before me and would help by translating my English and his French. Ionesco was short and bald and somehow so compressed that his slightest change of expression seemed an explosion of feeling. He was not just glad to see me, he was GLAD! In the dining room, Mrs. Ionesco had spread out a selection of cold herring, anchovies, clams, and shrimp with bread and aquavit. She was a tiny woman, pretty and compressed like her husband. She smiled: EAT! The language barrier between us pained Ionesco, but after several aquavits we seemed to communicate over and around the difficulty.

Anti-Americanism among European intellectuals, he said, was part of a malaise of self-destruction. And he wondered whether Americans did not themselves have a suicidal instinct that caused them to create anti-Americanism.

He said three or four selfish American capitalists would have done more for the people of Russia and China in the past forty years than either Lenin or Mao Tse-tung. Yet, while Soviet intellectuals are apologists, Western intellectuals habitually criticize.

Ionesco said he had spent six weeks in the United States battling against the idea that his play, *Rhinoceros*, was anti-American. American intellectuals wanted to believe it was an attack on conformity when it was really an attack on totalitarianism. Suicidally, they wanted to see an attack on the United States.

They also reveled in the idea of a theater of the absurd. Ionesco said he denounced absurdity. He worried, he said, about the loss of vitality in America, the loss of optimism, the loss of faith that good will triumph and that bad guys always lose.

At last, he wanted to know: Who *really* killed Jack Kennedy?